What People Say about
The Whale Done School

Schools are a major force in socializing the young. Educators recognize that basic perceptions and attitudes of our students are more divergent and less predictable than ever before. We are now addressing the widest range of individual differences known in history. Schools are actively seeking effective options for behavior education. The Whale Done School is a practical example of transferring theory to practice with impressive results. The book's examples and guidelines makes it a valuable resource for educators. Establishing a positive, respectful culture allows students and staff the benefit of focusing on learning in a healthy environment. Congratulations to the authors for this innovative approach.

Dr. Roberta DiLorenzo, Superintendent
Washington School District

We have been following the Whale Done philosophy in our school for the past three school years. Since we have caught the Whale Done wave, we have watched the atmosphere in the building transform with more respect and positive interactions. It has made a great difference in our building and the young children adore the consistent whale theme. Our Whale Done Wednesday morning presentations are the highlight of our school week. The students look forward to seeing if they will be recognized for their outstanding efforts, get "splashed" by their peers, and proudly wear a whale sticker for the day. I have also been excited to share the power of being positive with other administrators and community members.

Michelle Tomicek, principal
Principal, Canon-McMillan School District

D1403330

The Whale Done School and its emphasis on the power of affirmation has been an inspiration to our staff here at The Early Learning Institute. It seems that human nature is to look for what's wrong, instead of what's right. Finding the positive that lies within all of us, and celebrating and praising it, has helped my organization further its mission. We see powerful results in the lives of the children we serve.

Kara D. Rutowski, CFRE
Executive Director, The Early Learning Institute

The Whale Done School is a testimony to ingenuity and commonsense. What a brilliant yet simple way to build resiliency in kids and and teachers! I highly recommend this book to principals, teachers and parents.

Joanne Spence
Executive Director, Yoga in Schools

"Enlightening, refreshing and uplifting . . . useful for any school."

Charlene H. Newkirk, South Campus President,
Community College of Allegheny County

This book is about changing a culture, about seeing the good in others and affirming those innate qualities. It's about the persistance of a visionary leader who believed in the power of positive relationships, a staff that implemented the vision, a community that supported it and students that thrived in it. This is a story of hope and perserverance that will inspire you to explore how the Whale Done philosophy can change your school.

Joshua White, teacher
Pittsburgh Public Schools

The Whale Done School

TRANSFORMING A SCHOOL'S CULTURE BY CATCHING STUDENTS DOING THINGS RIGHT

Cindy Zurchin,
James Ballard
Thad Lacinak

authorHOUSE®

AuthorHouse™
1663 Liberty Drive
Bloomington, IN 47403
www.authorhouse.com
Phone: 1-800-839-8640

Published by AuthorHouse   09/12/2012

ISBN: 978-1-4685-9536-9 (sc)
ISBN: 978-1-4685-9537-6 (e)

Library of Congress Control Number: 2012907442

CONTENTS

This book is dedicated to all the teachers, administrators, staff members, students, and families who are helping to create schools where teachers love to teach, students love to learn, and parents can be proud.

If you treat an individual as he is, he will remain how he is. But if you treat him as if he were what he ought to be and could be, he will become what he ought to be and could be.

—Johann Wolfgang von Goethe

Introduction

For years I've been telling business leaders that the key to developing people is to catch them doing things right. Yet I still find that the number one way people know they're doing a good job is that nobody's yelled at them lately. Sadly, this "leave alone/zap" leadership style is not only practiced by managers in the workplace but by parents, grandparents, and teachers as well.

I have always firmly believed that punishment is harmful in human relationships. When I saw my first Shamu show in San Diego—where killer whales, the most feared predators in the ocean, had been trained to leap somersaults in unison, ride trainers on their backs, splash the audience with their tails, and accomplish all sorts of other feats—I was fascinated. Did the trainers punish the whales when they did something wrong and then get back in the water with them? Common sense tells you that this wouldn't be a smart move.

On a behind-the-scenes tour of SeaWorld® I learned that when a whale shows undesirable behavior, the trainers redirect the whale's energies back on what it was supposed to do and praise the whale when it behaves appropriately.

Inspired by this great example, I teamed up with SeaWorld's head whale trainer, Chuck Tompkins, his long-time colleague Thad Lacinak, and my good friend Jim Ballard to write the best-selling *Whale Done! The Power of Positive Relationships*. If the simple tools of building trust, praising, and redirecting could get five-ton whales to jump thirty feet in the air, we knew they would work with people as well. Knowing that what was good for whales and grown-ups would be good for kids, too, we next published *Whale Done Parenting*.

Given its power to change lives, I am so excited that the Whale Done philosophy has now been applied to schools, transforming them into places where kids can learn in a positive environment.

The story that follows is based on co-author Cynthia Zurchin's journey at Pittsburgh's Schaeffer

Primary School. Faced with rising rates of student absenteeism, suspensions, and declining academic performance, Cynthia encouraged teachers to apply the Whale Done principles of accentuating the positive, praising, and redirecting. Over the course of the next two years suspensions dropped dramatically, academic scores improved, and the school atmosphere changed from hostile to healthy.

With the exception of Thad Lacinak—who continues to play an important role in spreading the Whale Done philosophy—the characters in this book are fictitious. Yet the benefits of applying these principles are very real. We hope this book helps teachers and school administrators everywhere to create schools filled with joy and learning.

—Ken Blanchard
Coauthor of *The One Minute Manager*®
and *Whale Done!*

CHAPTER 1

A Rocky Start

"I won't have my daughter going to a school where she can't study, where she's being bullied, and where there are so many disruptions she can't learn. I might as well have her spend her days in a war zone!" The mother glared at the principal before sitting down with an indignant shake of her head.

Principal Maggie Carlson was presiding over several dozen parents and a half dozen teachers who had gathered in the Wildflower Elementary auditorium for the emergency meeting now in progress. Last week's merger with Lincoln Elementary had the community in an uproar. The looks on most of the parents' faces were as dark as the September storm clouds that loomed outside.

Still wearing his raincoat, another parent rose and said, "I don't know what kind of shape the district's budget is in, but this change makes me think there's a sneaky plan behind this move. Taking a quiet, orderly school like ours and merging it with kids from the projects—I'll bet they're looking for our school to fail so they can close Wildflower, too. What do you think, Dr. Carlson?"

Maggie Carlson took a moment to consider her reply. "We need to make the best of this change," she said calmly. "While the superintendent expressed some concern about the risks of the merger, he's confident that we can handle it."

Maggie was being diplomatic. In truth, the superintendent had offered her little support.

A parent shouted from the back of the crowded room, "Give us back our school!"

The cry triggered an immediate reaction. In one corner several parents began chanting the slogan:

"Give us back our school! Give us back our school!"

The principal recognized the mob response. She raised her hands and called, "Please, please!"

The room became quiet. Though small in size, Maggie Carlson commanded respect.

"I know you're upset," she said. "I have concerns myself. But what we have to realize—all of us together, right now—is that this decision is not going to be reversed. These students from across town have been added to our classrooms and as a result, our school's student body character has changed. That's the fact. Let's discuss how to make the best of it. A number of you have been challenging the district's verdict, and that's well and good. But it's time to get to work and take action on your concerns. What are your ideas?"

A woman in the front row raised her hand.

"Go ahead," said Maggie.

"The first problem we should handle is the fighting on the buses," the woman said, drawing nods from the audience. "We can't have every school day beginning with chaos even before the kids have reached class!"

"That's right," added a scowling father. "Kids are screaming and wrestling and throwing books and backpacks. The bus drivers have all they can do to keep the buses on the road. There's got to be supervision!"

"Agreed," Maggie said. "What's your plan, Mr. Bell?"

"I don't have one," the man replied. "Do you?"

Everyone looked at the principal. She took a deep breath. "We could have a group of volunteers ride the buses with the children. The rides could be scheduled, with volunteers signing up for once a week."

No one spoke.

"Or every two weeks, if enough people volunteer," Maggie said.

Still the room was utterly silent.

"Any volunteers?" asked Maggie.

Not a hand went up.

Maggie sighed and was about to give up when one of the teaching assistants spoke up.

"I could ride a bus," the assistant said. "I might be able to get several other teaching assistants to volunteer with me."

The nods and smiles in the crowd showed people's approval of this idea. Maggie made an effort to keep her eyes from rolling. As usual, it seemed the community would rather complain than take action.

"Thank you, Melissa," she told the assistant. Then she turned to the audience. Look," she said emphatically, "I am more committed to this school than ever before. In my book, failure is not an option. We're going to make the best of this merger. We will not fail."

CHAPTER 2

A Bad Situation Grows Worse

Despite Maggie Carlson's determination to make the best of the Lincoln-Wildflower school merger, over the next few months the fallout climbed to toxic levels. On a brisk winter morning she found herself coming to the rescue of a teacher with yet another unmanageable student.

"Thank you, Ms. Wissell. You can leave us alone now, please."

The shaken teacher hurried out the door looking more than glad to leave.

Maggie turned to the tall second-grader who stood before her. She noted the look of disdain and rebellion in the girl's face and the filthy, ill-fitting clothes she hugged around her as though she wanted nothing to do with her present environment.

"Karen," Maggie said, "this is the third day in a row you've been brought here. What's going on?"

The girl folded her arms across her chest and looked away.

"Ms. Wissell tells me you have a habit of running out of the classroom and beating on the hallway locker doors. We can hear it all over the school."

Maggie waited, but Karen ignored her, staring out the window.

"I know you can hear me," the principal persisted, "because I see you have a beautiful pair of ears." She waited a full minute, then said, "Maybe you just need a time outside of class. You can sit here quietly while I do my paperwork."

Twenty minutes went by without a word or movement from Karen, who sat staring out the window, her lips clenched in a resolute frown. Occasionally Maggie looked up and studied the youngster. *Who knows what this girl goes home to?* she thought. *She's like so many who are here at Wildflower now, shipped in from their destitute neighborhoods. Barely seven years old and she's doubtless seen enough drugs, violence, and abuse for a lifetime.*

A bell rang. Maggie rose to go supervise the lunchroom. Putting a hand on Karen's shoulder and feeling the thin body tense, she said, "Come on, let's go see what's for lunch."

On the way down the hall the two were met by Fran Wingate, the reading specialist. Fran's face held a sickly expression. "Think you'd better come with me," she told Maggie.

After handing Karen over to a teacher aide, the principal followed her team member to the boys' bathroom. As they approached the door, Maggie frowned at the stifling odor. After entering, Fran pointed to a sink. It held a pile of fecal matter. The two educators looked at each other in horror.

"I've seen kids pee on the floor," Fran exclaimed in disgust, "but who would poop in a sink?"

Maggie shook her head. "It just shows the level we're operating at with these new kids," she said.

Closing and barring the door to the boys' room, she called the custodian on her cell phone. "Harold, you're not going to like what you find in the boys' restroom. Clean it up and I'll owe you one."

Maggie had barely reached the lunchroom when third-grade teacher Vicki Middleton accosted her. "You hear about the fight in my room this morning?" she asked.

Maggie shook her head. "I was in a fight of my own with a father who came to school drunk in PJs and slippers," she said with mock cheerfulness. "What happened?"

Vicki's dark eyes flashed. "We were lucky not to have an ambulance on the scene. Mattie Nichols threw a chair at another student and barely missed his head. I had to step in between the two of them." She rubbed her forearm. "Those kids are strong."

Maggie took Vicki's arm gently in her hands. "Are you hurt?" she asked in a comforting tone.

"Not really," Vicki said, grinning. "But we may need a bouncer in this school before long!"

By the following spring, the situation at Wildflower Elementary had reached the breaking point. A second emergency school community meeting was called to discuss the deterioration of the school. The meeting room was crowded with grim faces. A smartly dressed woman rose from the crowd and the room grew hushed.

"Most of you know me," the woman said. "I'm Sue Norman."

Sue Norman had been instrumental in convening the meeting. A former PTO leader, she had been outspoken in her protest against the district's school reorganization plan. Her two children were top students and popular leaders. Now all eyes were on Sue as she faced the principal and the two team leader teachers sitting at the front of the room. Sue's tone was icy.

"Like most of you, I've been devastated by the effects on this school of this insane district reconfiguration. Last summer some of us organized to fight the decision, to no avail."

From the rapt attention of the crowd, it was evident that people looked to the speaker for guidance.

"I love Wildflower," Sue said. She paused and cleared her throat. "That is, I loved it at one time. But things have changed so much these past six months that I no longer recognize this school when I walk into it. That's why I'm taking action on my own. Considering the sad state the place is in now, I have no recourse but to remove my children from it. I am enrolling Jake and Emma in a charter school over in Walton."

She stood with her hands crossed over her chest. An uncomfortable silence filled the room.

"The rest of you can do as you please. I'm through." She sat down and a pall fell over the audience. The meeting broke up minutes later.

CHAPTER 3

A Ray of Hope

"That's the lowest blow yet," Maggie Carlson told her husband that evening. "When parents like Sue Norman pull out, they take the best students and families with them."

Roger Carlson patted his wife's arm lovingly. Their two children were in bed and for the past twenty minutes they'd been discussing Maggie's challenges over tea at the kitchen table.

"It looks bad all right," Roger said, "but honey, I have never known you to back away from a fight."

"You kidding? I have no intention of backing away," Maggie said. "It's just that, there goes our parent leadership team in one fell swoop. I don't know any individual in the community I can count on now. And I'm at my wit's end to know what to do about these incoming students. We can't just get tougher on them. Every time I'm forced to suspend a kid, I go against my own best values. I didn't become an educational leader just to spend my time keeping the lid on things."

The two sat silently for some minutes.

"This will probably go nowhere," Roger said, "but I'll offer it anyway. In our managers' meeting today Phil told us about a new book."

"Another one, huh?" Maggie said without enthusiasm. "Your boss is always looking for new management ideas."

Roger nodded. "Anyway, this book looks to be different in at least one respect. It's by a top management consultant who says that to increase people's motivation and productivity, leaders should adopt the same principles they use to train killer whales!"

Maggie blinked. "What does whale training have to do with management?"

Roger caught a hint of interest in his wife's manner. "That's the thing Phil's most excited about," he said. "It's all about ignoring what people do wrong and recognizing what they do right. The idea is that what we focus on is what we get more of. Phil says that's the way they train the whales, and the same technique can be applied to people. He calls it *catching people doing things right.*"

Hearing that phrase, something inside of Maggie jumped. "What's the name of this book and where can I get it?" she asked.

"It's called *Whale Done! The Power of Positive Relationships,*" said Roger. "Phil gave us each a copy. I've got mine here in my briefcase."

That evening Maggie completely submerged her mind in the ideas of *Whale Done!* The book wasn't long but she lingered over the chapters, frequently taking notes and highlighting passages. Her mind was in a whirl as she applied each principle to her situation at Wildflower. Every part of the book was feeding her growing vision for school-wide change.

Whale Done! tells the story of Wes, a business manager who is not getting along well with people at work or with his teen-age daughter at home. Taking a break from a business conference, he visits Marine Life Parks, International. He's amazed by the relationship between the giant black and white killer whales—the most feared predators in the ocean—and their trainers. The whales appear to be not only willing but eager to perform: leaping and diving, splashing the front rows of spectators on command, sliding onto the deck, and waving with their flippers on command.

Thinking he might learn some secrets to help him improve people's performance back at work, Wes stays around after the show to ask the trainers how they achieve such cooperation. He finds out that the key to the whales' peak performance is building trust. The trainers downplay the whales' undesirable behavior and focus on praising and rewarding them for what they do right.

Around midnight Roger found Maggie still reading in the living room.

"You're really into that book," he said.

Maggie's eyes were shining. "It just might hold the key to solving the issues we're having at Wildflower," she said. "The main character of this book finds out that the same principles trainers use to get 10,000 pound whales to cooperate can be applied to human relationships in the workplace. He sees that so many managers don't even notice when their employees do what they're supposed to do, but when mistakes occur they quickly jump on them and send *gotcha's*—blaming and punishing messages. When he starts focusing on what people do right and praising them for it, he succeeds at work and at home—and has a lot more fun in the process."

"You think this applies to school and kids as well?" asked Roger.

"I do," Maggie said. "Children have a built-in need to be recognized for their goodness. I believe that deep inside, every student at Wildflower—including the so-called hard cases—needs to be seen as lovable and capable."

"Pretty hard to see kids as loveable when they're throwing chairs at each other," Roger opined.

"That's just it," said Maggie. "We're always focusing on what the kids do wrong. We spend very little energy calling attention to what they do right. This book says you always get more of what you pay attention to. Which means we've been doing it exactly backwards at Wildflower! Maybe focusing on the positive is the solution."

"Maybe so," said Roger.

CHAPTER 4

Learning a New Way

Several teachers had gathered in the faculty room, waiting for a staff meeting that would start at the top of the hour.

"Larry Adler's threatening to quit again," Joanne Wissell said.

"Oh, no," said Vicki. "Larry's our oldest bus driver. He's been here since before I came to Wildflower."

"Well, you can't blame him. We're not providing enough staff people to ride with all the buses."

Shawn Treadway, the physical education instructor, spoke up. "The place we need more coverage is the lunch room."

"You got that right!" said Ruth Gomez, a first-year teacher. "That fight yesterday was a disaster. It seems like when two kids start up, a whole bunch more want to get in on it."

"Reminds me," Shawn said, "of an old Irish saying, 'Is this fight private, or can anyone get in it?'"

There was a lull. Then someone said, "Anyone know why Maggie's called this meeting?"

Vicki looked at her watch. "All I know is, I've got to take my son to the doctor, so this had better be quick."

A kindergarten teacher named Bella came in and sat down with a heavy sigh.

"Anyone have any suggestions for keeping the noise down in your classroom?" she asked.

The question was greeted by chuckles, rolled eyes, and comments like, "Good luck!" and "Have you tried taping mouths shut?"

Bella said, "I expect five-year-olds to be chatty, but this bunch just shouts. I think all they hear is noise at home, so they don't know how to talk normally."

"Hi everyone!" The small talk ended as Maggie Carlson entered, smiling and carrying a large box. The remaining staff members came in behind her and took seats.

Maggie set the box on the table. "Thanks for coming," she said. "I know this isn't our regular staff meeting time, so I appreciate you all showing up."

"What's it about?" a tall teacher with a perpetual frown asked. "I have to be somewhere." No one was surprised at Dorothy Hairston's challenge.

"A special thanks to you, Dorothy, for joining us," Maggie said. Her tone was warm and sincere, without a hint of sarcasm. "I have something really important to share with you and it can't wait.

"Ever since the school year started we've been wrestling with the results of the merger with Lincoln Elementary. We had a nice, quiet, orderly school up to last fall. Now we're tearing our hair out every day just trying to keep our school from falling into total chaos. We've tried all kinds of measures to keep order. I think you'll agree with me that nothing has worked."

"We know all that," Dorothy said in a surly tone. "So what's this important thing you have to share?"

"Thought you'd never ask," Maggie said, grinning. She opened the box in front of her, took out a copy of a shiny blue and white book, and held it up. "*This* is what's new," she said firmly. "This little book, *Whale Done! The Power of Positive Relationships*, is going to be our guide to turning Wildflower School around!"

Maggie wasn't surprised to see the teachers looking around at each other skeptically. She went right on. "When I read this book, I realized that something has been right here staring us in the face all along, and we were so caught up with trying to maintain order that we completely missed it. The heart of the change that will take place here at Wildflower is a shift in our own attention."

"Excuse me, Maggie," said Sarah Quinney, a young teacher everyone liked. "Could you just give us the bottom line? In a nutshell, what is this big secret that's going to save us?"

Maggie grinned. "It's this." She picked up a marking pen and turned to the whiteboard. As her team watched, she wrote:

Catch students doing things right.

Before others could comment or question her, she went on. "It's calling on what the subtitle of the book says: the power of positive relationships. It's about shifting our attention from what students do wrong to what they do right. It's making a science out of recognizing the good in kids."

"Yeah, right," said Dorothy Hairston in a tone of contempt. "Show me something a kid around here does right."

"Cut it out, Dorothy," Sarah said. "I like this idea. I want to hear more about it."

The principal smiled. "Thanks, Sarah. But I don't plan to talk to you any more about it. I want each one of you to read about it." With that she started unloading books from the box and passing them to each side, to be distributed around the table. Soon everyone had a copy of *Whale Done!*

"This book is not long," said Maggie. "It's written in story form. Most people would call it a quick, easy read. But good things, as you know, come in small packages. This book holds the key to turning this school around. As you go through it, keep on applying everything you read to our situation at Wildflower. When we come back together here at our regular meeting on Tuesday, I want everyone to have finished reading the book. We'll talk about it then. Have a good rest of the day, everybody."

"You think because you're a principal you can push people around. I don't give a damn about you being a principal! I'm telling you I want to know why my child can't get out of school to go with me to court to testify against my husband!"

If the woman's imposing body seemed to fill up most of Maggie's office, her loud voice took care of the remaining space. Maggie took a moment to internalize her attention. She felt her heart speed up. She recognized the twinge in her chest as a first sign that she was entering fight-or-flight mode. But she took a breath, smiled, and spoke in a calm, low voice.

"Thank you, Ms. Raymond, for taking the time to come to school. We always appreciate our parents visiting here."

Momentarily put off by her failure to provoke a fight, the woman paused. She quickly resumed her bullying manner, although some energy had been lost.

"I don't care about your fancy words. I *will* have my daughter out of here at noon today, or you'll be sorry. You don't want to see my brother coming in here! You think *I'm* bad, my Lewis will make you sorry for messing with me."

"I would like to meet your brother, Ms. Raymond," Maggie continued, unfazed. "He is welcome here anytime. I always like to meet the family members of our students."

Irene Raymond was on unfamiliar ground here. Accustomed to seeing her victims cower before her imposing size and pugilistic manner, she was nonplussed at being spoken to in a kindly way. Her bravado had run out of steam. Her mouth opened, but nothing came out.

Maggie Carlson rose and moved around her desk. "As I've told you, Ms. Raymond, if you bring a written order that your child is to appear in court, I will see to it she goes with you," she said pleasantly. She moved toward the door. "Thank you so much for sharing your thoughts. I'm sorry to cut our visit short, but I need to supervise the lunchroom."

Her visitor stood up and walked to the door. "I guess I'll be back with the order," she murmured.

Maggie was reflecting on the interview as she went down the hall. Her mind was full of wonder. *I don't believe this*, she thought. *If I hadn't read that book I'd have taken a much different approach.*

Later that day, the principal was eating lunch with some of the staff in the teachers' lounge. Ruth Gomez was telling her, "I couldn't put that book down last night—"

Just then Dorothy Hairston entered the room. She went to the refrigerator, pulled out a paper lunch bag and a can of soda, and took a seat across the table from the two. She avoided eye contact as Ruth continued.

"It's so fascinating," said Ruth, "how they take the science of training killer whales apart for you and show you why it works."

"Yeah, I learned something, too," said Ted Dorman, the music specialist. "Now I know what A-B-C means." He gave Ruth a challenging look.

"Okay, what?" Ruth asked.

Confidently Ted pronounced: "Antecedent, Behavior, Consequence. It shows that it's what you do *after* a person acts that makes the difference whether the action is repeated."

"I haven't read the book," Dorothy broke in. "I haven't read it, and I'm not *going* to read it!"

The room was silent. Everyone looked at Maggie. The principal smiled.

"Thanks for sharing that, Dorothy," Maggie said pleasantly. "You have a way of expressing your thoughts very clearly."

At closing time that day, three teachers were talking together in the parking lot.

"I don't blame Dorothy one bit," said one. "This Whale Done solution Carlson is proposing is useless."

"I read the book," said a second, "but I don't see how it's going to make a difference. These kids are too hard-core."

The third teacher spoke up. "Right. This isn't the school I signed up to teach in. Come spring, I'm out of here!"

CHAPTER 5

The Kickoff

The following Tuesday the assembled teachers were trading stories as they waited for the staff meeting to begin.

"I walked by a student and could see the lice crawling in her hair," said Nora Kidder.

"Terry Finley threw up all over my desk this morning," Patricia Meese said.

Sarah challenged with, "I had a father barge into my classroom yesterday, grab his kid, and kick him out into the hall."

"I've had that happen before."

"Yeah, but did your parent take a *belt* to the kid?"

"Okay, here's Maggie."

"Glad to see you," the principal began. "Hope you're all using lots of vitamin C against all the kids' colds going through the school. This place can be full of germs. Let's get started. I'm going to have us postpone our discussion of the holiday program until next week so we can concentrate on Whale Done. Did everyone read the book?"

Heads nodded around the room. No one looked at Dorothy; her negative response was a given.

"All right. Let's hear what some of you think about instituting a Whale Done program here at Wildflower."

For the next twenty minutes the group traded opinions about the reading and what it could mean for the school. As Maggie had expected, there were some who saw a process of steady praising as being ineffectual. Some openly doubted that it would change anything at all. Right away they wanted to know if they were to just ignore what kids did wrong. Conversely, a good half of the teachers were ready to try the new method.

As Ruth Gomez put it, "What have we got to lose? The District has tried all kinds of plans and rules and complicated matrices in the past. They've even called them 'positive approaches', but they always focused on the negative. They've wasted thousands of dollars—and none of them have worked!"

Finally, Sarah turned to Maggie and said, "I think you need to tell us what you're expecting us to do."

The principal took a deep breath and made her announcement.

"I'm glad to have all your opinions, but in this matter I'm prepared to go all the way," she said. "I know it's going to take a lot of work, but I am declaring Wildflower under siege. The attack is to begin immediately, and the weapons are Whale Dones."

Maggie turned on her laptop and the screen at the front of the room lit up. "Look at this," she said.

The image was of a simple but attractive certificate:

Whale Done!

This is to certify that

_____

has completed requirements for this
special award by doing the following:

_____
_____

_____   _____
Teacher's Signature   Date

"We need a tangible way to reward students. Each of you will get a stack of these Whale Done certificates. I want you to start handing them out whenever you see a child doing something rewardable."

"What's 'rewardable'?" asked Vicki Middleton, the third grade teacher.

"It can be anything. We don't want to make Whale Dones cheap, but at first I think we need to be pretty lavish with them, if only to get them out there showing up, so kids want one for themselves. For example, if you've got kids that don't stay in their seats, you can start rewarding the ones who do. Whenever you catch one student in an act of friendship or kindness or generosity—any of the behaviors or attitudes that we want to bring out more of—give a Whale Done."

"So you'd write the kid's name, but where it tells what it's for, what would you write?"

"Anything you want."

"'Showing kindness?'"

"Right. Or, 'helped another student with a math problem.' In fact," said Maggie, "let's brainstorm right now a list of things a student could earn a Whale Done for. We're looking for positive, desirable behaviors in students—all the while ignoring, as best we can, the poor or undesirable behaviors."

For the next few minutes the principal wrote items the group named. The list included:

turning in homework	being a friend
sitting quietly	helping someone
raising hand	sharing
being quiet	getting along with others
talking quietly	cleaning up
coming to school	listening
coming on time	smiling
lining up	being happy
making friends	being careful
waiting your turn	being neat

As the group reviewed their list, a loud sigh was heard from the back of the room. It was Dorothy. "Just wasting more time," she said.

Maggie countered, "Hey, with the way things are going, we can't afford not to take the time! So, let's call this a partial list. The point is, you can give a Whale Done for anything a child does or says. In terms of strategy, I've thought about two uses of these awards. One is to catch kids who are already doing things right, and make them examples. The other is to watch so-called problem kids for a time when they're doing what they should be doing, then jump in and surprise them with a Whale Done. In both cases, we want kids to feel good about what they've done so they want to do more of it—and also to provide incentive for other kids to think, 'Hey, I'd like to get one of those.'"

"How do you get the word out?" asked Vicki.

"Yeah," said Sarah. "I was wondering: Is the kid who receives a Whale Done the only one who knows about it, or maybe just other students in the classroom where it happens?"

Maggie frowned. "I'm not sure," she said. "I want to make the launching of the Whale Done program a big deal, a real celebration."

"Let's make Whale Done announcements over the P.A. system," someone said.

"Good idea. The kids eat breakfast here every day. Why not do it at that time?"

Dorothy spoke up. "Yeah, right. You could hold an assembly every morning to announce these Whale

Dones you're talking about," she said sarcastically. Her eyes flashed as she looked around. She had meant her comment to sound absurd, but the teachers were staring at each other thoughtfully.

The principal read the agreement in her team's response. "Not bad, Dorothy!" she exclaimed. "That will certainly let all the kids in on what we're doing."

"It will make daily school-wide stars of kids!" said Ruth, glowing with the idea. Soon the group was talking excitedly.

"We'll need a certain amount of bookkeeping for this," said Peter, ever the organizer. "All Whale Done certificates will have to be turned in at the end of each school day for the next morning's assembly."

"Turned in where?" someone asked.

"To . . . me, I guess," Peter said, grinning.

"Maggie can read them aloud each morning in the assembly," Sarah said.

"And when kids come up and get them," Maggie added, "instead of clapping, we'll have all the kids call out, 'Whale Done!'"

"We can decorate the cafeteria with beautiful killer whale stuff," said Martha Wooding, the art teacher. "I can get those projects going right away."

As the planning went on, more staff members jumped in with ideas. Soon the white board was filled with items. They were organized under such headings as *school activities, parent communications, local news*, and *community promotion*.

"One more thing," Maggie announced as the meeting was coming to a close. "I want each of you to prepare an action plan of your own for implementing Whale Done. It shouldn't just be through certificates you fill out to reward kids. For each of us, the biggest change that a successful implementation of this program will require is a change in the way we see kids. The work will be in what you watch for. I want us to be positive in our relationships with each other, as well as with the students. I want the spirit of Whale Done to permeate this place each and every day.

To start with, I want each of you to think right now of three people to whom you'll give some sort of a Whale Done—a compliment, an unexpected thank-you, some kind of recognition for something they've done right. This could be either here or outside of school. Personally, I'm going to give one of mine to my son Jason—a Whale Done for shoveling our walk faithfully every snowfall.

"My second Whale Done I will present privately to a teacher. For my third, I'll have to think about it. I might just call my boss to recognize her for leaving me alone and staying out of my way!" This brought chuckles.

"Whale done, everybody!" Maggie exclaimed, ending the meeting. Turning to Dorothy, who was rising to leave, she added, "And a special Whale Done to Dorothy, who got us off on the right foot!" Dorothy hurried out of the room to a chorus of "Whale Dones!"

After the others had left, Sarah said to Maggie, "Some of these teachers are going to take a while to get on board."

"Sure," Maggie agreed.

"Aren't you worried about the resistance?"

Maggie grinned. "Hey," she said, "resistance is a whole lot better than indifference. At least when there's resistance, you've got something to work with."

CHAPTER 6

Better than Homeless

"Trey, get in here and clean up this mess your sister made!"

The boy, dressed only in a T-shirt and jeans despite the wintry cold, was sitting on the steps of the old house next door to the building that contained his mother's tiny apartment in the housing project. He rose and went inside, his nose wrinkling at the acrid smell from a leaky propane heater.

Keira, his two-year-old sister, her mouth and chin glistening from her runny nose, played on the floor amidst a scatter of broken toys, empty cigarette packages, and soiled clothing. Trey bent down and went through the motions of straightening up. His mother Lola, as usual, was talking on her cell phone.

"That judge doesn't know what the hell he's talking about," his mother was saying into the phone. "Albert says he wasn't even there! . . . I know. I have to appear with him next week. I don't know what to do. I can't get anything done." She pulled the phone from her ear long enough to tell the boy, "Her diapers need changing, too, honey."

Trey pulled his sister to her feet, led her to Lola's bed, and cleared away the piles of dirty clothes. He lifted her to the bed—the boy was strong for his eight years—and began the changing process. He made faces at his sister to entertain her. Keira giggled at him and drooled. Trey could hear Lola going on with her ritual worrying by phone. He wondered whether Albert, his seventeen-year-old half-brother, would be released from jail this time.

As he cleaned the mess, Trey tried not to think about last night. He was accustomed to being kept awake most of the night by the shouts and laughter from the house next door, just as he was used to the ache behind his eyes from the propane fumes. His mother's boyfriend Rudy—called Shooter by his friends—always had a crowd over. As on other nights, last night's partying had grown loud and raucous. Then, just after two a.m., a sharp explosion brought Trey sitting upright.

A shot, he thought. *That was a shot!*

Unable to sleep, he lay there trembling until, hours later, Lola shouted, "Ty, we're out of cereal. Go ask Rudy to give you a box."

The boy's heart skipped. "I'm not feeling good, Mama," he complained. "I think I'm getting sick."

"I think you're *fine*!" Lola's warning was unmistakable. "You get back here with those Cheerios in a hurry or you'll miss the bus."

Trey made his way across the concrete space that separated his home from the house next door. The dark low tenement building brooded over its weedy lawn. He knocked timidly at the door. Curtains parted at the window and Rudy's face, ravaged by hangover, appeared. He mouthed the words, "Go around back!"

Trey shrugged and held out his hands, saying, "I'm right here. Why can't you—"

Rudy's face hardened into a scowl the boy knew only too well. Deciding he was just as happy not to view the scene beyond the front door, he turned and went around the side of the house, picking his way past the cheap plastic chairs, strewn garbage, broken toys, and a dead, discarded Christmas tree. Catching sight of him, a huge pit bull leaped at Trey from behind the chain-link fence. The dog's ferocious barking and repeated jumping at the jangling fence sent terror through the little boy.

"It's okay, it's okay," he pleaded, trying not to look at the slavering jaws and vicious red eyes of the animal.

The weathered side door opened and he was glad to enter the house. The place smelled of stale beer and something else. In the kitchen gloom Rudy's huge form loomed. Dressed only in underwear, he lit a cigarette.

"Whatcha need, kid?"

"You got Cheerios?"

Rudy opened a cabinet and pulled out a big box. "Your mom doin' okay?"

"Yeah," said Trey, reaching for the box. "She's fine."

Rudy held it back. He leaned down until his face was close to Trey's. The boy could smell the rank odor of his breath. "Tell me something, kid," the man said in a voice that was almost a whisper. "You hear anything around here last night?"

"No, I didn't hear *nothin'*!"

The man stared at him.

Knowing the way he answered had sounded suspicious, the boy looked helplessly at the floor. He felt a huge hand on his shoulder.

"Good. Now you get back home. And tell your mama I said hey."

"Hi, Trey." Nick Laird greeted his friend as he came down the aisle of the bus. The two always occupied the seats over the rear wheel, as these were shunned by the bigger kids.

Trey stood in the aisle as the bus was pulling away, looking at the dirty yellow building where for three years he, Lola, and Keira had occupied a dark and cramped apartment. His mind uttered a silent opinion it had repeated many times: *At least it's better than when we were homeless.*

Pandemonium reigned during the ride to school. Trey and Nick huddled together, ducking as books, pencils, and other items hurtled around them, thrown by shouting students who ran about the bus and climbed over seats as the driver vainly shouted threats and warnings.

A fight broke out at the back. The boys were not surprised to see that Mattie Nichols—the one they called the Kicker—had just sent another boy to his knees, holding his crotch and crying pitifully.

Mattie came down the aisle, smiling. As he passed Trey the bully jeered, "What're *you* looking at?"

Trey and his friend were glad to reach Wildflower Elementary without further trouble. The moment the bus stopped the boys joined others squeezing and pushing as they piled off and ran for the school building.

"No running!" "No pushing!" the teachers called after them.

As the children reached the front doors, the teachers shepherded them toward the cafeteria. Trey felt a surge of anxiety when he realized he was not going to his classroom. Routines were so rare in his life that he unconsciously clung to them. He wondered what was wrong. When he entered the cafeteria he was awed to see giant black-and-white inflatable whales hanging from the ceiling. The front stage area was decorated with an ocean motif. What fascinated him most was the movie scene on the huge screen at the front, in which huge glistening, black-and-white shapes—killer whales in pods—moved gracefully through the sea.

The young audience was mesmerized.

Sarah had rented a nature documentary from a local store and arranged for it to be projected, with the sound turned off. Another teacher had set up a CD to play the sounds of ocean waves over the cafeteria speaker system. With the ocean white noise as background—and two hundred students giving the whale video the trancelike attention they gave their TV "babysitters" at home—the cafeteria was eerily quiet.

The principal, Dr. Carlson, stood up in front of the room and faced the crowd. The video and sound effects faded.

"Boys and girls," she said, "this is the first of many times we will gather here at the start of a school day. As you look around, do you see something different? It's whales, isn't it? These beautiful animals are called killer whales. Maybe some of you know about them from television and movies."

"Now, how many of you have heard someone say 'well done' to someone who did a good job on something?"

Some hands rose and several children called out or murmured responses.

"Good," said Maggie, "I thought so. We are going to be taking an idea from a book about killer whales called *Whale Done*. It sounds like 'well done,' doesn't it? So we will be telling you all Whale Done when you do something right."

She held up a certificate. "This is called a *Whale Done*, after these beautiful whales. It will be given to one of you as a way of saying 'Well done' for something you did that was good. We'll be proud of you when you earn a Whale Done, and you'll be proud, too."

The room was quiet as the kids absorbed the message.

The principal continued, "Now I'm going to call out the names of some students who will each receive one of these special prizes today. As I call your name, please come up and get a Whale Done with your name on it. Afterward, we'll all show that person our appreciation."

Maggie read from a list that had been compiled the day before, based on the teachers' observations of these students' actions.

"Darryl Landry gets a Whale Done for walking quietly in the hallway."

The little boy came, grinning sheepishly, while the others stared.

Handing him the award, Maggie said, "Now, I want everybody to give Darryl here a special Whale Done. This is how it's done. First, I want everybody to take a deep, relaxing breath."

Around the room was the sound of air rushing into lungs as Maggie and the children took a deep, collective breath.

Maggie turned to Darryl and said enthusiastically, "Whaaaaale, Done, Darryl!" Then she addressed the students. "Let's all try it."

All over the cafeteria the voices rose with the principal's: "Whaaaaale, Done, Darryl!"

The ritual was repeated as Tanya Fox received her Whale Done for helping the teacher clean up after art class. George Williams got one for helping another student with a science project. And on it went. The crowd stared as they watched their classmates come forward and be recognized. Again and again they were prompted to add their own congratulations with the Whale Done cheer.

When she finished calling the dozen or so names, Dr. Carlson said, "You boys and girls who received these Whale Dones should be proud you have earned them. Be sure to show them to your families when you get home today. All of you will be taking a letter home today, explaining to your parents about our new Whale Done program of showing how proud we are of the good things our Wildflower students do."

As the teachers led the groups of students to their classrooms, Maggie looked again at the take-home letter she had composed. It read:

Dear Parents and Guardians:

I am very excited to share with you a behavior changing program that we're going to be using at Wildflower Elementary. The program is called *Whale Done!* It highlights techniques used by whale trainers at Marine Life Parks, International, who discovered that you can't get a 10,000 pound killer whale to jump 30 feet in the air by screaming at it or punishing it. A positive reward for proper behavior is the only thing that works.

Children, too, respond better to praise and rewards than to punishments. I am asking for your help in keeping the children's focus on doing the right thing. Use these *Whale Done!* strategies with your child at home:
- Praise your child right away when he or she does the right thing.
- Tell your child what he or she did right or *almost* right.
- Encourage him or her to keep up the good work.
- When your child misbehaves or acts out, don't scream. Give him or her time out to cool down. Then replace the poor behavior with another activity he or she is allowed to do.

I've attached some *Whale Done!* certificates for you to use with your family. Please tell your relatives about the *Whale Done!* program, too. Together we can make sure that Wildflower Elementary students continue to be successful and are able to take advantage of the college scholarships that are waiting for them through the Education Promise. For your cooperation in advance I say, *WHALE DONE!*

Sincerely,
Margaret Carlson
Dr. Margaret Carlson
Principal

CHAPTER 7

Managing the Change

For the rest of the day after the Whale Done assembly in the cafeteria, Trey kept noticing little indications of a change in the atmosphere of the school. It was as if he and his classmates were being watched in a new way. He felt it everywhere—in the classroom, in the hallways, in the lunchroom, on the playground. There had always been teachers in those places, but they had not been so . . . watchful.

In the classroom Ms. Middleton, his teacher, kept saying things like, "That's a nice smile, Ella," or "Are those new shoes, Ralph?" or "Deena, thank you for being a good materials manager in your math group," or "I sure like how everyone is sitting quietly and doing their work!" Trey wasn't sure he liked it. You couldn't always be sure what the big people were up to.

A few days later he was sitting in the cafeteria watching Dr. Carlson hand out Whale Done papers to his fellow students. Suddenly he heard his friend Nick's name called. He watched Nick go up and get his Whale Done. Then he joined in the chant following the awards: "Whaaaaaale done, Nick!"

Later Nick proudly showed him his award.

"It says here I was good because I shared my book with another student," Nick said.

"That was me," Trey said. "I forgot my book at home yesterday."

"Right," said Nick. "I didn't even know the teacher saw that." He smiled as he looked at his Whale Done. "I'm gonna have my mom get me a frame for this and put it up on the wall at home."

When the school day ended, the two friends had another surprise. Ms. Keeley, the kindergarten teacher, boarded the bus with the students. Before they started off, she stood up in front and said, "Boys and girls, I like the way you're all in your seats. Let's try to keep it that way during the ride home."

When they'd gone a few blocks, Mattie, the boy known as the Kicker, got up and walked down the aisle to where his friend Bobby was sitting. Everyone looked at Ms. Keeley, expecting her to yell at Mattie. Instead, she gave the boy a firm stare, then looked the other way. Mattie showed off to the others by laughing and carrying on with his friend. As he started back to his seat, the teacher turned and smiled warmly at Bobby. Then she announced, in a voice everyone could hear, "Bobby, I am proud of you for keeping the rule of staying seated while the bus is moving. You'll be getting a Whale Done at tomorrow's assembly."

That was when it dawned on Trey. *The teachers aren't just being nice to you for no reason,* he thought. *They're watching everybody to see who should get a Whale Done.*

At the staff meeting on Friday, Maggie was pleased to hear encouraging comments from the staff about the new effort.

"I can see changes in some kids already."

"I've seen them show more respect to the ones who get the Whale Dones."

"I think it's working," said Debra Kindall. "Stella, my noisiest kid, actually came to me today and asked me if I thought she could get a Whale Done for being quiet."

"What did you tell her?" Maggie queried.

"I looked mysterious and said, 'I think there's a chance, but I'll have to see you working at it."

"Good," said Maggie. "That's an example of negotiating for a Whale Done."

"It's called a bribe!" taunted Dorothy from her corner.

Maggie looked thoughtful. "No," she said after a pause. "A bribe is paying someone to do something or not do it. This came from the child. It's got self-motivation to it, and that's what we're trying to build. I think it's perfectly okay for kids to want to earn a Whale Done by changing. That's the whole idea behind the whale training."

Somebody remarked teasingly, "It's in the book, Dorothy."

Bella Keeley spoke up. "I've got a new system for giving Whale Dones to share with you. I started off having the kids call out "Whale Done!" when a classmate did something right. But then they were doing it all the time. After a while it became a distraction. There was so much noise in my classroom, I thought, 'Have I created a monster here?'"

Several teachers were nodding their heads, indicating they were having the same problem.

"So here's what I did," Bella continued. We talked about how the killer whales swim by pumping their flukes—their tailfins—up and down. And we agreed on an arm motion"—here Bella held up her arm and undulated it in a fluid motion—"as a way to give a silent Whale Done. It works fine. The kids like to do it, and there's no noise."

"That's a great solution, Bella," Maggie said. "I think we should all adopt it. Let's have the undulating arm movement be the official way to acknowledge good behavior and performance in Wildflower classrooms. We'll reserve the cheer for our group assemblies."

The teachers agreed it was a good idea.

Maggie said, "Before we close the meeting, I wanted you to know that yesterday I made a call to the director of animal training at Marine Life Parks, International. His name is Thad Lacinak and he's one of the authors of the book *Whale Done!* I told him about what we're doing here and he got excited. He said he'd like to visit the school and see for himself how we're using the Whale Done principles. I told him he'd be welcome. We set a tentative date for December, when he can stop by on his way to visit his family over the holidays." Maggie could see her news had sparked enthusiasm among the staff.

"Hopefully, by the time he visits we'll have made a good start on getting Whale Done embedded in our school culture," Sarah said.

"I want Thad to meet with our staff when he's here," Maggie said. "From our conversation, I think we have a good friend in this man, and a future consultant and champion of our program."

One day in math class as the children were working in groups on problems, Trey's group finished early. As their leader, he went up to the teacher's desk to turn in his group's answer. As he stood before the math teacher, Ms. Hurley, she reached out to him. He felt a momentary pressure on his chest. Looking down, he saw the image of a beautiful leaping killer whale attached to his ragged sweater.

Ms. Hurley beamed at him. "Congratulations, Trey," she said. "You're one of the first students to receive a brand-new Whale Done sticker. This is the first one I've given out. You deserve it for your good work in here and for being a responsible leader of your work group." She instructed the class to take a relaxing breath and then led them in the undulating Whale Done Wave.

Trey hurried back to his seat, feeling the eyes of the whole class on him. He could hardly concentrate the rest of the morning. He was thinking how his mother's face would look when he showed her the prize.

At recess he saw Mattie, the feared predator of the school, standing with some of his friends. The bully waved him over. Ignoring Mattie was not an option. Trey slowly advanced until he stood before the boy. He felt sick inside as he anticipated one of Mattie's signature kicks coming at him.

"So," Mattie said, "you got a big whale sticker there, huh? Let's see it." He snatched the sticker away and turned to his friend Bobby. "Dog, you look like you could use a Whale Done sticker." He pressed the prize onto Bobby's arm. The latter, in turn, peeled it off and stuck it in another boy's hair. Soon they were pushing each other and laughing, passing the sticker around.

Trey watched helplessly as his beautiful prize fell to the ground and was trampled by the scuffling boys. When the bell rang, the bully retrieved the sticker and came over to him.

"Here you go," Mattie said. "I guess it got a little messed up." Tossing it at the boy's feet, Mattie ran off with his buddies to the school building, laughing.

Trey picked up the wadded-up mess and peeled it open. Torn and creased, the sticker now had dirt and grass stuck to the back of it. He was too embarrassed to go ask his teacher for another one. With a heavy heart, he sighed as he looked at the sticker. He didn't think he would be showing it to his mother now.

On Tuesday the students were gathered as usual in the cafeteria for the morning assembly. Dr. Carlson was reading the list of students receiving Whale Dones for that day and the honored students were coming forward one by one to receive their awards and be cheered by their classmates in the now-traditional Whale Done assembly chant.

As the ceremony ended there was a momentary lull. A small hand went up in the back of the room. Maggie acknowledged it, and all turned to see Sam Wainright come to his feet with a big smile. One of the few original student body leaders whose parents had resisted the exodus and had kept him at Wildflower, Sam was liked by all. Knowing he had everyone's attention, the boy turned deliberately to face the imposing figure of Dorothy Hairston.

"I want to give my teacher, Ms. Hairston, a Whale Done for giving me extra help in math," Sam said.

Following the boy's warm and sincere tribute, Dorothy's face was in shock." Gradually, the rigid scowl melted and tears gleamed in her eyes.

Amazed by Dorothy's transformation, Maggie was speechless. During the pin-drop silence that ensued, she recovered enough to grab a blank Whale Done form, scribble Dorothy's name on it, and hurry to the back of the room.

"Here is your Whale Done to give to your teacher, Sam," she said loudly enough for all to hear. "Shall I write 'for helping me in math'?"

The boy nodded.

"Now, we'll write in today's date and you sign it here," Maggie finished.

When Dorothy took the paper Sam offered, her lips were trembling. "Thank you, Sam," she murmured.

Around the room, tears glistened in teachers' eyes.

"Boys and girls," Maggie announced, "What do we say at a time like this?" She led the resounding cheer, "Whaaaaale *Done*, Ms. Hairston!"

CHAPTER 8

Whale Done Catches On

"Show went well, don't you think?"

"Hm. About an eight, I'd say." Thad Lacinak, chief animal trainer at Marine Life Parks, International in Orlando, Florida, was measured in his praise. "I think we can get tighter between the announcer's preps to the audience and those synchronized front flips."

"Right." Laura Smolls agreed with a grin. "But don't you *love* seeing Kusti's flawless timing?"

Thad smiled at Laura's enthusiasm. She was one of the trainer-performers in the killer whale show and he knew she wouldn't give up her job for anything. Having helped Marine Life Parks, International pioneer the training of its killer whales, Thad had experienced the thrill of working with these intelligent creatures many times over the years.

The two were standing next to one of the backstage pools watching the great killer whales move slowly through the water.

"Love those guys!" she said, her eyes sparkling. "Gotta go give Quadra a rub-down to show her what a champ she was this morning. Have a good one."

As Laura headed off, Thad began his usual inspection tour of the facility. Strolling around the side of the pool, he was thinking of the phone call he had received yesterday to an elementary school principal in Detroit named Dr. Maggie Carlson. She had told him she was instituting a school improvement program based on the book he'd coauthored, *Whale Done! The Power of Positive Relationships*. That book had been aimed at a business audience and Thad had been contacted by a number of organizational leaders who had found its methods useful in turning their companies around. But this morning's call was different. It had alerted him to an instance where Whale Done principles were being used to change a troubled school. The call had excited him—so much so that he told her he would like to visit her school.

As he walked, Thad noted a young whale named Taat in the far corner, eyeing him eagerly. He was already behind in his morning rounds, but Taat and he had a special relationship. The youngster had been born in his presence here just over a year ago, so he had a real fondness for the little fellow. He tapped the surface of the water and Taat swam over to him. The whale lifted its head, stuck its tongue out, and nodded to him. Thad knelt and rubbed the young whale's great soft tongue.

"There," he said. "You like that, don't you, boy?"

Finishing his caress, Thad rose and continued on his way. In an adjacent pool he watched two trainers working with Panya, an older female whale, to clean her huge teeth with a whale-sized water-pic. Around the corner he waved to two other crew members who were filling fish buckets for the morning feeding. In yet another area he watched a trainer named Dwight treading water out in the middle of the pool. Dwight was working with a beautiful whale named Kaa-Shaade, one of the top show performers. He was signaling Kaa-Shaade to break dance after her slide-out, but she was missing his cue sometimes. Thad noted how Dwight redirected those times that the whale was off, but patted her back enthusiastically when she did it almost right and rewarded her with a treat when she perfected it.

Continuing on to the area they called the Whale Salon, he inspected the equipment there, making sure the whale lift was clean and the area was well supplied with the tools used to take periodic urine samples and conduct health exams as needed to the whales. He checked the chart on a clipboard briefly, to see that his office records coincided with them.

In a way this morning's tour was a trip down memory lane for the head trainer. Over his more than twenty years at Marine Life Parks, International he had been instrumental in putting most of these procedures in place. Remembering his talk with Maggie Carlson again, he was glad that the complicated behavioral science theories on which MLPI's animal training was based had been pared down to three simple rules that could be applied to humans of any age or background. He was eager to help Maggie launch a Whale Done program at her struggling school. Her vision and enthusiasm inspired him.

Thad started back to his office. Approaching the building, his eyes went to the sign above the door, the one that summarized the steps that were faithfully followed in all training of the killer whales:

> - Build trust.
> - Accentuate the positive.
> - Redirect when necessary and reward desired behavior.

We've been at this so many years now, he thought, *and still the rules never change. You get more of the behavior you pay attention to, so pay attention to good behavior.* His mind returned to the phone call he'd been contemplating. *What a difference these simple steps could make if teachers consistently applied them!*

Darryl yelled at Trey across the aisle of the school bus. "Did you watch *Cops* last night? Whoa, that one scene when the cops' car went off the road was cool!"

"Ssh, keep your voice down!" Trey said quietly.

"What's the matter, man? You afraid we'll get in trouble with Ms. Singleton?" Darryl nodded toward the teacher in the front seat.

"No," Trey said. "Just don't be so loud!"

Since the bus now always had a teacher on it during his rides to and from school these days, Trey thought he might score a Whale Done by being quiet and staying in his seat. Now that most of the students were obeying the rules, it was harder to stand out. His shushing of Darryl came from his not wanting to attract the teacher's attention to their part of the bus. In the days and weeks since the loss of Trey's precious sticker at the hands of Mattie, he had been consoling himself by determining to earn a Whale Done and be recognized in the morning assembly. Even though his mom had missed seeing his Whale Done sticker, he would still make her eyes light up by presenting her with a certificate suitable for pasting into her old scrapbook.

It had been a long time since Lola had pulled out that scrapbook and looked at it with him. Trey had treasured those times of snuggling up to her on the couch as she turned the pages, looking at pictures and talking about happier times when his half-brother Albert was small. One entry was a faded newspaper clipping showing Albert and his basketball team when they won the district championship. Albert had been the top scorer in the playoff game. Those pictures always made Trey want to do something to make Lola proud of him, as well. Maybe his earning a Whale Done could make his mother feel better during this time of stress when her mind was never far from Albert's trouble.

By the time the school year came to a close, the Whale Done program was really catching on. At lunchtime in the teachers' lounge, staff members were beginning to share what they called "the good stuff" instead of the most alarming incidents. They were also trading ideas for recognizing students.

"The arm signal has really caught on in my classroom," said Nancy. "Every time a student gives a right answer, the arm-swimming starts."

Ted said, "The stickers are really going over well, too. I have to be careful not to cheapen them by giving out too many."

"I agree. Three a week is plenty."

"I've got kids researching killer whales," Ted said. "They seem to bring in new facts and stories every day."

CHAPTER 9

Word Spreads

As the new school year began, word started to spread about the new program at Wildflower Elementary. Maggie wrote about the Whale Done program in the district newsletter. She also started a blog called *Whale of A Story* in which she reported the good things teachers and students were doing at the school. Early comments on the blog were for the most part positive:

> You are doing something wonderful at Wildflower. I am glad to see that a public school finally recognizes the power of affirming students. I am sure you will soon see the impact of your Whale Done Program on student achievement.
>
> —A parent

> My child was thrilled to receive a Whale Done certificate. We have framed it and hung it on her bedroom wall. Thank you also for the letter home,

encouraging parents to back up your good work by calling attention to what our kids do right.

—Louise Kendry,
teacher aide in District 7

The program was not without its critics.

I read about your school. Looks like the inmates have taken over the prison.

—Anonymous

One day the principal received a phone call from Myra Allred, a reporter on the local newspaper *The Sentinel*, wanting to visit the school and write an article about the change. Maggie welcomed the attention. She also knew there were many other schools out there who had lost hope of ever creating a school where teachers love to teach, students love to learn, and parents were proud.

A week later, Myra toured the school and interviewed the principal. Her article was the first of several to let the community know about the changes taking place at Wildflower School. Myra was so impressed with the school—the warmth that pervaded the classrooms, the caring attitude of the students—that her article was glowing.

Middletown—March 15.

There are two words you hear spoken again and again at Wildflower Elementary these days: *Whale Done!* This play on the familiar compliment is also the name of a new school improvement program launched by the principal, Dr. Margaret Carlson, and her staff. Walking through the halls of Wildflower, one sees inflatable whales hanging from the ceiling and miniature whales sitting on students' desks. Banners remind students and staff to "have a whale of a day."

The Whale Done program recognizes student achievement—not only for academic performance, but for good behavior as well. Carlson has instituted a program of praise to help resolve the student problems that resulted when the Lincoln Elementary School was merged with Wildflower after the district's closing of 20 of its schools. With 93% of the Lincoln students living below the poverty line—in an area where residents are on probation or parole—teachers say that demographics made for a volatile mix in the classroom.

Carlson is basing her program on *Whale Done! The Power of Positive Relationships,* a book that describes how the principles used in training killer whales can be applied to managing people in business environments. Carlson believes the book's methodology holds the key to healing the school's woes. "Instead of concentrating on the things students are doing wrong," Carlson says, "we reversed it and started noticing and rewarding them for their good efforts."

The program appears to be paying off. Suspensions have been reduced from five per week to less than one. Reading scores have begun to improve. Tardiness rates have dropped significantly—in part, Carlson believes, because students want to get to school on time to attend the morning assembly where "Whale Done" certificates are awarded for good behavior. Teachers report that fights and bullying have all but been eliminated. "Watching the kids' smiles and their pride," says Dr. Carlson. "It's obvious these kids thrive on praise."

The article stimulated positive responses from the community. Several parents asked how they could help. Two teachers phoned Maggie at home from a department store in the city where there was a big sale going on. They wanted to buy mittens and scarves for the kids and wondered how many they should get.

Soon the Kiwanis Club was offering money for school supplies. Then a global coffee chain jumped in to make a donation. One local business bought every child a coat. Hospice volunteers came and entertained for a show, collecting funds to give each student a book bag. The CEO of J&N Industries, Inc., a former teacher, stepped forward with a generous donation.

The community optimism was infectious. It seemed everyone wanted to give a Whale Done to Wildflower School. Everyone, that is, except the school district itself. No one on the staff had heard any mention from central office about the program. Despite the community interest, it seemed Wildflower's improvement was being studiously ignored by the administration. Then one day three people from the district arrived without notice. Maggie first spied them walking down the main hallway. "May I help you?" she asked.

"I'm Dr. Anderson," said a tall woman in a condescending voice. She could not seem to make eye contact with Maggie as she talked. "We've been inspecting the school and have some questions."

"I'm Dr. Carlson, the principal here," Maggie said firmly. "Are you saying you've been touring the school without coming by the office to check in with me first?"

Dr. Anderson smirked. "We're like the secret shoppers the department stores use," she said. "We wanted to see what was *really* going on here."

Maggie made an effort to curb her anger. "And what did you find was '*really* going on'?" she mimicked.

"We just stuck our heads in the doors of a few classrooms," said the man on Dr. Anderson's right. "It didn't seem that much was going on at all."

"Not much discipline, anyway," said the third. "It looks like teachers here are just trying to be nice to everyone. I saw students calling out answers without raising their hands. A couple hadn't turned in their homework on time but they weren't reprimanded!"

To Maggie they all sounded like quacking ducks—and she had heard enough quacking.

"If you'll allow me, I think *you* are the ones who didn't do your homework. Did you ask any questions of any teachers? Did you try to find out what's behind the way they are treating the kids? How do you expect to grasp what our teachers are trying to do by simply poking your heads in, interrupting classrooms, and looking for what you think is wrong?"

"Dr. Carlson," the leader said in a chilly tone, "we came here to ask *you* questions, not to be asked." She consulted her notepad. "To begin with, why is this whale theme repeated so often throughout the school? We can understand an art project or science unit devoted to an animal species, but isn't this going overboard?"

Quack, quack, quack, thought Maggie.

"I must apologize for leaving," she said sweetly, "but as you know, I had no idea you were coming. I'm afraid I have a meeting to attend." She pulled a copy of *Whale Done!* out of her briefcase. "Please accept this copy of our guidebook. If you read it, I'm sure it will answer most—if not all—of your questions."

With a parting smile she turned and walked away, leaving the inspection team speechless. "Who knows, you may even pick up some tips on giving effective feedback."

"We've heard about your new program, and want to know if we can come and visit to observe it in action on a school day." This request came to Maggie by phone from a charter school principal. It was repeated by the head of a Montessori School, so Maggie arranged to have the two groups visit on the same day, and to arrive in time to witness the morning assembly.

On the day of the visit, two administrators and seven teachers stood at the back of the cafeteria as the Whale Dones were handed out. Afterward they visited several classrooms where teachers demonstrated the Whale Done techniques of affirming students. At the end of their tour, the group convened in Maggie's office.

"This is fantastic!" one of the visitors told Maggie in wonder. "We thought this was some nationally known, structured program that you had adopted. Now we realize you and your staff have created this entirely on your own."

Maggie picked up a copy of *Whale Done!* "Not entirely on our own," she said with a smile. "This was our guidebook. I hope you all will read it if you're thinking of starting your own programs."

"My plan is to do as you did," said the middle school principal. "I'll buy a copy for every staff member and go from there. I hope you don't mind if we simply copy the techniques—the stickers, the decorations, the arm signal, the Whale Done certificates."

Maggie laughed and said, "By all means, be our guest! We want to see Whale Done spread all over our own district, so why not into yours?"

As the group was leaving, one teacher stayed behind.

"Can I speak with you alone?" she asked.

"Sure," said Maggie.

When the woman opened her mouth to speak, her eyes filled with tears. "I've been having such a hard time with discipline this year that I'd decided to quit teaching. But now that I see what you're doing here, I'm going to stick it out."

Maggie put a hand on the woman's shoulder. "I'm sure those killer whales will be glad to know they've averted their first teacher casualty!" she said with a smile.

CHAPTER 10

Turnaround

Ever since Dorothy Hairston had received her Whale Done from Sam, both her students and fellow teachers had noticed a change in her. For the first time there was laughter coming from her classroom. Students began to come around her desk for help. In the old days staff members received no eye contact or words of greeting when they passed her in the halls. Now she met them with sincere smiles. Before long, Dorothy volunteered to ride the bus with the students. And one day she told Maggie quietly, "I read the book."

One morning two students in Dorothy's class started yelling and pushing each other in the back of the room. Dorothy quickly intervened, moving them apart and asking them to think about what they'd done. Several minutes later she sat down at their table with them.

"Now, Kara and Elroy," she said with a smile, "you are turn-and-talk elbow partners, and in my classroom turn-and-talk elbow partners get along. I see there's a disagreement, but I've also seen how kind and thoughtful each of you can be."

The boy and girl looked at their teacher helplessly. Their wide eyes said that they were no match for her—she obviously had something up her sleeve.

Dorothy said, "Kara, you've been telling me all about your cat. You said he—what's your cat's name?"

"Tom."

"Tom, that's right. Tom was sick the other night, wasn't he? And what did you do? You stayed up with him and held him until he felt better. That was so nice."

Dorothy turned to the boy. "And Elroy, you know how to be a good friend, too. I was in the office at recess time the other day when you came in with your friend Rusty. What happened to him?"

"He fell and hurted his knee."

"Yes, that's right, and you put your arm around him and brought him in and sat there while the nurse worked on his sore knee, didn't you?"

Elroy wore a small smile as he nodded. Both he and Kara had obviously forgotten their fight. Their anger had melted in the face of Dorothy's kindness and sincerity.

"I'm going to leave you two nice people to work together now," Dorothy said as she got up, "because I know you both know how to be good friends."

For the remainder of the period Elroy and Kara worked together amiably on their project. As the class was filing out past the teacher's desk, Dorothy called them to her.

"I saw how nicely you worked together," she said. "Thank you."

"You're welcome, Ms. Hairston," they chorused shyly.

After they left, Dorothy made a note to write up Whale Dones for Kara and Elroy for the next day's assembly.

Four teachers were talking together in the teachers' lounge.

"Did you hear that mother carrying on and threatening Dr. Carlson in the office this morning?" said one teacher. "Honestly, I wonder how these kids survive in their homes with their own parents."

"I can't even imagine what some of my students are up against when they leave school," said a second.

"There is such darkness where these kids come from," a third teacher said. She turned to the teacher who had been silent. "How do you deal with the darkness in your classroom, Dorothy?" she asked.

Dorothy thought a moment. "If you're in darkness, it doesn't do any good to start punching at it. So, what do you do?"

The others sat, musing.

"Bring in the light," Dorothy said. "Then the darkness just goes."

"Right," said Vicki. "But where do you *get* this light that will dispel the darkness in these kids?"

Dorothy looked surprised. "Why, Vicki, the light is already there in the children!" she said.

Nowhere was the change in Dorothy more evident than in her complete embrace of the Whale Done program. Whale Dones were coming in consistently in her handwriting. She made suggestions for adding features to the program that left other teachers thinking, *Why didn't anyone think of that before*? Dorothy's forcefulness—formerly laced with barbs and sarcasm—was now aimed in a positive direction.

One day the staff was discussing the growth of community interest in the Whale Done program.

Dorothy said, "Everybody just wants to feel good. When they find something that makes them feel good, they want to be part of it."

The teachers nodded in agreement.

Dorothy's eyes grew bright. "We should have a Whale Done Celebration!" she said.

Maggie said excitedly, "Great idea, Dorothy! As a matter of fact, Elizabeth Harrison, the CEO of J&N Industries, came to visit the school after she read the article. She made a donation, saying that the kids should be rewarded for the positive changes in their behavior. I'll call Elizabeth and see if she'll sponsor a Whale Done Celebration."

The idea met with enthusiastic approval from the staff.

"Meanwhile, let's get busy putting our individual Whale Done plans into action. At our next staff meeting

I want everyone to report on the progress they've made in their classrooms."

The next staff meeting was a lively one.

"I transferred a happy whale cartoon I created into a rubber stamp for marking papers," said Martha Wooding, the art teacher. "If any of you want one for your class, I'll be happy to make you one."

"My students are designing their own Whale Dones to give to friends," said Sarah Quinney.

"I'm giving Whale Dones to my players for good sportsmanship and team play," said Shawn Treadway, the PE instructor.

"At first I couldn't see how catching kids doing right could possibly help the discipline in my library," said Ellen Talbot. "But after giving Whale Dones this past week, the library is a much quieter, but somehow also livelier place."

While the consensus about the program was positive, teachers also shared their difficulties with the program.

"Catching kids doing right is really hard for me to do," one of them said. "It's a complete shift of attention. There's no sitting back to relax."

"That's true," another agreed. "It's more work because it's counter-intuitive. It goes against the way we were trained as teachers."

"Maybe even more important was the way we were taught by our own teachers when we were kids," added another.

"Don't forget that you don't have to wait to 'catch' kids," Dorothy put in. "I say things like, 'I'm looking for the students who are sitting nicely at their table,' or, 'Look at this part of the line, how these students are standing ready to go.'"

Before the meeting ended, Maggie told the staff, "Larry Adler, one of the bus drivers, said he's seen a big improvement in safety since teachers started riding our buses with the kids. From now on we will pick the teachers up at home, to make it easier for them to ride the buses with the kids."

"That's great," said Maggie. "And it gives me an idea: Let's give Whale Dones to entire busloads of kids when they ride peacefully for a whole week."

Late one afternoon when most teachers had left the building, four people lingered in the office area. Dorothy stood at the mail boxes talking with Nora, a second-grade teacher known for her capacity for gossip. Maggie and her assistant Jane were seated at a nearby table, going over some district reporting forms.

Nora was carrying on about Harold, the school custodian. "I can hardly stand that man," she said. "I make some simple request—like for him to clean up some extra mess for me after we've done a project in my classroom—and he looks at me as if I've asked him to move the world. I wish he would bathe once in a while. And I certainly hope he doesn't use the kind of language I've heard from him in front of the boys and girls."

Dorothy listened silently as Nora complained. When Nora finally stopped, Dorothy looked puzzled and said, "That's strange. Harold has spoken to me so kindly about you. He has a lot of nice things to say about you."

With that, Dorothy went to the sink, washed out her coffee mug, said goodbye, and left. Looking thoughtful, Nora soon followed her out the door.

Jane, who had overheard the conversation, said to Maggie, "I don't think I've ever seen such a complete turnaround in a person as I've seen in Dorothy. How do you account for her being so utterly resistant to the Whale Done program, and suddenly being a model for us all in carrying it out?"

"We both know what triggered it," Maggie said. "We all were there when she got Sam's Whale Done."

"But I'm talking about how she's been *since* then," Jane persisted. "She's like Whale Done personified!"

Maggie was thoughtful a moment. Then she said, "I saw a similar thing happen once before and I have a theory about it. When someone is completely against an idea the way Dorothy was, it reminds me of Shakespeare's line, 'The lady doth protest too much.' Certain people are constituted in such a way as to be completely loyal to something, once they've embraced it. Thus, they may fight it because they're cautious about what they'll give their all to. It takes a lot for them, but once they're on the other side of the fence, they're totally and irrevocably behind it."

"That's interesting," said Jane. "If all teachers knew about how that works, they might look at resistant students in a whole new way."

"Right," agreed Maggie. "The thing is, you don't know how to trigger the turnaround. It probably takes something purely of the heart and unexpected—like in Dorothy's case—something that catches the person completely unaware and open."

"That's it," said Jane. "One little word and bingo! You never know when a person is ready."

CHAPTER 11

Celebration

As the holidays approached, reading tests conducted at Wildflower School confirmed improvement at all grade levels in reading scores. Maggie was keeping close tabs on these. She envisioned a time when a study could show a correlation between academic improvement and Whale Done teaching procedures. She reported the higher scores to the district, but no attention was paid to them. One day she received an e-mail from her boss, assistant superintendent Helen Lowry. It read:

> You are to report to the superintendent's office on Friday at 2 p.m.

Maggie put in a call to Helen. "What's this about?" she asked.

"It's to answer questions about why your school is failing."

"What do you mean, failing?" Maggie asked indignantly. "Failing how?"

"Just show up," Helen said.

"No, Helen. I won't just show up. Tell me what this is really about."

There was a long pause.

"If you must know," said Helen, "they're looking to close more schools to cut costs. Wildflower's a code red school."

Maggie took a deep breath. "I'll be there," she said.

Four people were present at the meeting in the superintendent's office on Friday: superintendent Derek Bond, assistant superintendents Helen Lowry and Angela Sterne, and Maggie.

"Let's get started," said Superintendent Bond.

"Sir, I don't mean to interrupt," Maggie said, interrupting. "I'd like you all to take a look at this." She quickly gave everyone a printed sheet.

"What's this?" asked the superintendent.

"It's an agenda," Maggie said. "I've prepared a presentation to analyze the situation at Wildflower School. May I proceed?"

The superintendent appeared both surprised and pleased. "Yes, go ahead," he said.

Maggie opened a laptop computer and set it on the table with the screen facing her audience. She used her remote to begin a Power Point presentation.

"I've prepared a root cause analysis of the situation at Wildflower School," she said. "This first diagram shows the various strengths of the factors involved in the change in our school culture."

For the next twenty minutes her listeners were treated to a series of graphs and charts, including those showing increased attendance, lowered tardiness and suspensions, a projection of the improvement already shown in reading scores, and the narrowing gap between white and non-white student achievement.

Throughout the presentation the superintendent was silent. As Maggie finished with a graphic of Wildflower's future academic performance trajectory, he turned to his assistant superintendents and asked, "Why is she here?"

Helen mumbled, "Uh, sir, she's here because you told me you wanted to see her."

"What's wrong with you?" he thundered. "You know what I mean! What in the name of heaven is a bright, intelligent, forward-looking and totally committed school leader such as Dr. Carlson doing spending a Friday afternoon in my office defending the outstanding job she's doing? Why, she's done more work than any other administrator in this district."

Turning to Maggie he said, "Where have you been? I think you're the smartest person in the district. If we had a dozen others like you around, maybe we'd see some positive results in our city's education program."

"Thank you, sir," Maggie said.

As she packed up her things to leave, she handed a copy of *Whale Done!* to the assistant superintendents, who both looked as if they were suffering from indigestion. "I highly recommend you read this," she said. "I know that you, as administrators, are committed to education. I think you'll find some truly helpful ideas in the book."

Maggie headed for the door. "Have a great weekend!" she said with a parting smile.

Eileen Moore, the activities director, gladly took on the job of coordinating the Whale Done Celebration. Because the winter holidays were coming up, she tied the event to the gift-giving spirit, getting the word out and making appeals to retailers and community organizations.

The school was so busy in the weeks before the year-end vacation that Maggie compared it to a bustling bakery shop. "Just take a number," she would say when people came crowding into the office with donated packages or to ask questions regarding the upcoming event.

Staff members spent long hours wrapping gifts for each child. Once a teacher complained that she didn't have time for gift wrapping. The look she received from Dorothy Hairston apparently re-enrolled her.

When the big day arrived, classes ended early and everyone gathered in the cafeteria. A huge banner proclaimed the event as the WHALE DONE CELEBRATION. Dorothy instructed the teachers to have their classes seat themselves in circles on the floor. Parents, media people and representatives of the participating businesses and community organizations stood around the perimeter, watching. Using a wireless microphone, Dorothy welcomed everyone.

"What is Whale Done, anyway?" she asked. "There could be many answers to that, but let's find out from the children what they think." Turning to the circles of students, she asked, "Who has an answer?" She went to a girl whose hand was raised. "Brenda, will you stand up, please, and tell us what Whale Done is?"

Brenda beamed and spoke into the microphone. "Whale Done is something you get that makes you proud."

Some adults began to clap, but their applause was silenced as the entire student body called out, "Whaaaaale *Done*, Brenda!"

Dorothy made her rounds among the circles of students, interviewing child after child who wanted to contribute. The adults joined in the acknowledgement chant each time.

Joe, a second-grader, said, "Whale Done is feeling happy."

"I like Whale Done," said kindergartener Marianne.

Karen said, "Whale Done makes me smile big."

A girl named Lizzie was particularly vocal about Whale Done. "Whale Done is being good and being noticed for it," she said. Dorothy made as if to take the microphone away, but Lizzie grabbed it back. "When I see my little brother being bad, I tell him, 'Hey, that's not Whale Done behavior.'"

After interviewing a few more students, Dorothy said, "Now I'm wondering who can tell us three reasons why all you students should get a Whale Done today." This part of the program was pre-planned, and Dorothy chose one designated student in each class to answer the question.

Randy said, "I think I should get a Whale Done today because I've helped my teacher, I've made a new friend, and I've stopped picking fights."

Tanya said, "I deserve a Whale Done because I've worked hard on my spelling, I've never been late to school, and I've read stories to kindergartners here."

Brad reported, "I should get a Whale Done for keeping my seat on the bus, staying away from trouble-makers on the playground, and raising my hand in class."

On it went, until Dorothy called for every student to stand and repeat a pledge she had prepared for the students to recite together:

I pledge to look for the good in everyone, to be happy and help others, and to follow a Whale Done way of life.

"Part of our pledge is about how we treat others," Dorothy said. "Right now I think each one of you boys and girls has something to give someone. Please take out the Whale Dones that you have written, and deliver them to your friends!"

Students bustled about, exchanging their written acknowledgements. Since the mass exchange had been carefully orchestrated ahead of time, with each class drawing names out of a hat, the entire procedure took only a few minutes. When the exchange session was over and children were seated again, a quiet, thoughtful period ensued as they read their Whales Dones from their friends. Soon the cafeteria was glowing with proud smiles and sparkling eyes.

Dorothy made a point of looking around. Then she said "The smiling faces I'm looking at everywhere tell me something: Giving and getting Whale Dones is all about *being happy*!" Then her eyes widened and she exclaimed, "Now it's time for presents!"

Suddenly teachers were rolling shopping carts, brimming with brightly wrapped gifts, to the circles. Each child's eyes were big and bright as she or he received a hoard of packages. All sat clutching their armfuls of gifts until every student had received a bundle.

Dorothy said mysteriously, "I wonder what's in these presents?" She paused to let the excitement build. "It's time to find out!" she exclaimed.

With that, she started the countdown that the children had practiced in their classrooms. The entire Wildflower School student body chanted, "Ten! Nine! Eight! Seven! Six! Five! Four! Three! Two! One! Whaaaaaaale DONE!"

What a fuss there was then, as the sound of tearing paper and ripping packages mingled with the cries of delighted children. Each child received a coat, mittens, a knitted hat, and a backpack—all of the right size.

After all the gifts were packed up, Maggie stood and called for everyone's attention. She said, "There is one person here whom none of you know yet. He came in while our celebration was going on and has been standing at the back of the room enjoying the show. I want to introduce him to you. Mr. Lacinak, will you come up here?"

A tall, athletic man in his forties came forward, smiling and waving to everyone.

"Boys and girls, this is Mr. Thad Lacinak, who's come all the way here from Orlando, Florida. Do you know what Mr. Lacinak does for a living? He trains killer whales!"

With that, the screen at the front of the room lighted up and a movie began. Gasps and cheers broke out from the students as they recognized the man before them as the wet-suited person hugging a huge whale in a pool. A series of clips followed, showing Thad feeding a whale, rubbing one down, and massaging the tongue of another. Next, the audience was treated to film clips of the fantastic killer whale show. They watched whales leaping and diving, waving their flippers at the audience, and soaking the front rows with sheets of pool water.

When the film ended, Maggie stepped forward.

"Mr. Lacinak helped write the book that started our own Whale Done program here at Wildflower. He will be here tomorrow to speak with us at our morning assembly and to visit you in your classes. Now, the buses are waiting but before we leave, we need to show our appreciation to our master of ceremonies Ms. Hairston, and to Ms. Moore, who organized this celebration—as well as all the teachers, parents, and others who helped so much."

With a huge smile, Maggie led the cheer. "Whaaaaale Done!"

CHAPTER 12

Whale Done Theory

The following morning, Thad and Maggie were visiting in Maggie's office when third-grade teacher Vicki came in leading a rebellious-looking student by the arm. "Sorry to interrupt," Vicki said, "but Mattie kicked *two* boys in my class this morning. I think he needs a suspension—or at least a time out!" Breathing hard and looking disgusted, Vicki turned and left.

The principal shook her head. "Mattie," she said, "we've got to find a way to keep you here for a whole day." The boy merely sneered and looked away.

"Come with me," Maggie said, getting up from her chair.

The youngster followed her into a small meeting room.

"Sit down here now, for a while," she said. She shut the door, went back to her office, and sat down at her desk with a sigh.

"This is a real problem kid," she told Thad. "The other day he was sent to me for pushing another boy's face into his cereal bowl. But his specialty is kicking other boys. None of the teachers can deal with him, and I don't do much better. Most days I just end up removing him from the classroom, so he spends a good deal of time here."

"What do you know about his home situation?" asked Thad.

"No father around, but he lives with violence just the same. I see his mother pull up outside in the car some mornings with him, and the two of them are going at it, swatting at each other and yelling and cussing."

"So he gets to school and takes it out on the other kids, eh?"

Maggie nodded. "It's pretty sad."

Thad thought a while. "It can be hard to redirect that kind of behavior," he said, "but it's worth a try. I wonder if we could get through to him with a Whale Done."

"Nothing else has worked," Maggie said.

"Okay for me to go get him?"

"Sure."

Thad went to the room where Mattie was sitting.

"Come on back to the office, son," he said.

When the boy was back in Maggie's office, Thad knelt down until he was at eye level with him.

"I want to ask you something," he said. "Do you *like* being sent to the principal's office like this?"

The boy shrugged and looked away.

"Is it fun being in trouble? I mean, don't you get tired of having Dr. Carlson call your mom and having them come to the school for a meeting? Wouldn't you rather spend your time with all of your friends?"

Mattie made no response.

"Look at me, son." Thad waited until they had eye contact. "You know what a Whale Done is, right?"

Mattie nodded.

"Do you think you could earn a Whale Done?"

Mattie frowned. "No way I will ever get a Whale Done! I am not a good kid."

Maggie's eyes watered as she remembered the times she had seen this young man's mother pulling him out of the car by his hair, kicking him, and calling him names. She had alerted the child welfare authorities, but their case loads had probably been too great to answer the call.

"You know," Thad said, "I'll bet you could get a Whale Done if you tried." Turning to Maggie he asked, "What do you think it would take, Dr. Carlson?"

The principal appeared to contemplate the question. Finally she said, "I think if Mattie went one period without kicking anyone, he could earn a Whale Done."

"How about it?" Thad said. "Do you think you could go one period without fighting?"

The boy shrugged, but his eyes were gleaming.

On Friday afternoon following the Whale Done celebration Thad was addressing the staff of Wildflower School.

"I know you've all read the book," he said. "I understand that some of you have overcome your initial refusal to read it and have even become scholars of it." He winked at Dorothy, who smiled. "Dr. Carlson has asked me to review some of the theory anyway. It never hurts to revisit the rationale behind what you are doing every day in your Whale Done approaches, to make sure they're most effective."

Thad looked around at the group and smiled. "Teaching is challenging, I know. So is training killer whales. We need to be very scientific and consistent when we are training an animal, and I would guess it's the same when you are working with kids. I want to see how you've been working with the Whale Done concepts. To start with, who can tell me about the A-B-C theory?"

Ted eagerly raised his hand.

"Go ahead," said Thad.

"A-B-C has changed the way I teach," Ted said. "The letters stand for Activator, Behavior, and Consequence. The Activator is whatever stimulates the Behavior you want. Say you're teaching basic multiplication in math. The Activators would be the actual instructional things you do. Suppose the kids are learning their fives tables. Maybe you start with manipulative objects—marbles or pictures of sets of five. Maybe after that you get more conceptual by having kids practice counting by fives—5, 10, 15, 20, and so on. Then you have them discover, hopefully in some fun way, that one 5 makes 5, two 5s make 10, three 5s make 15, and so on. Those discoveries are all key Activators. So are the out-loud drills and the chances you give students to practice on paper or worksheets. By these means you're trying to stimulate B, the Behavior you want, which is the kids' ability to use the times tables accurately to multiply those numbers.

"These A and B parts are familiar stuff to all of us," Ted continued. "We remember teachers having us do activating exercises—A—so we could get to B—learning math, for example. Traditionally, we as teachers have put all our attention on A—the lessons. We've always worked to improve them, because we thought that the lessons or Activators were the only things that caused students to want to learn the Behaviors—doing math. But Whale Done theory has shown me how important the C—Consequence—is in effective learning."

"Say more about that," urged Thad.

"If kids get a positive Consequence after they demonstrate the Behavior we want—in other words, after they learn a certain math skill or concept—they'll have a positive attitude toward learning, which makes them want to learn more. Attitude toward what is being learned is vitally important. All of us know that you can teach kids to *do* math and at the same time teach them to *hate* math. And you can do the latter without even trying!"

Around the room, heads were nodding.

"It's that C—what we do *after* we get the Behavior we want from a student or class—that we have to pay the most attention to. Before we learned about the Whale Done approach, I was just walking the kids through the lessons—A/teach—followed by B/kids' learning. I was leaving out the all-important

C—reinforcing each move in the right direction by giving a Whale Done. Now I'm always looking for what kids do right. I consistently reinforce students' progress with either a verbal Whale Done, a Whale Done arm motion, or something else that makes them associate learning with feeling good."

"Wow, nice going, Ted," said Thad. "You've not only laid out the A-B-C theory, but you also shared how it's impacting your practice as a teacher. Great!"

The teachers spontaneously gave their acclaim. "Whaaaaale *Done*, Ted!"

"I love this," said Thad, smiling. "I can get you guys to do all the work! Okay, let's see if somebody else can review the four kinds of responses."

Lucy, the science teacher, raised her hand and was called on. She rose and went to the whiteboard. On it she listed:

1. No Response
2. Negative Response
3. Redirection
4. Positive Response

"There's a lot to be said about each of these responses and their effects," Lucy said, "but I'll go through them pretty fast. The first, the No Response— is the total absence of any acknowledgement, positive, negative or neutral. It's the most common response of all. It's also the deadliest. All of us humans are like the killer whales we read about in *Whale Done!* We want attention. We want to be noticed. Children that experience the No Response often 'act out'—they misbehave because that gets them *some* attention. By the time they're adults, most people have learned to live without being acknowledged. It's like people say about where they work: 'The only time they notice us is when we screw up!'

"Ted covered the importance of the Consequence. Parents, teachers, managers, and bosses don't realize what they're doing when they leave that out.

At its worst, receiving no response to what you do right from someone you want to please or succeed for, can send a silent message—*You are unimportant. You don't count.* Or even: *You are invisible. You are not even there.*"

Maggie put in, "Excuse me, Lucy. You teachers know what we are dealing with. Lots, or even most, of the kids who go to school here live with this lack of response. At home they're abused and punished, neglected, and ignored. Most of them are left on their own to play in the streets."

Lucy continued, "Going on to the Negative Response, we call this the *Gotcha*! It means, 'Hah! I caught you doing something wrong.' Most people in charge of other people—parents, teachers, coaches, bosses—tend to think it's their job to correct others when they make these—" Lucy wrote on the white board:

Misteaks

Her audience chuckled.

"So," she said, "as you look at what I wrote here, what do you want to do with it? Can I go on here with our discussion, or will your minds continue to be bothered by having that misspelled word up there?"

The teachers laughed as they realized Lucy had caught them thinking just that way.

"Correcting mistakes is only part of the job," she went on, "but it can easily color the way teachers see their students or parents see their kids or bosses see their employees. They begin to see them only as *people who need correcting.* When you were in school, did your teachers have you exchange quiz papers and correct each other's? And what were the instructions they gave for how to mark the papers?"

"Put an X next to the wrong answers," someone said, to nodding heads all around.

"Exactly right. So out of ten questions you could have nine correct and one wrong. Now, what were you told to write at the top of your classmate's paper you were correcting? Was it the number right or the number wrong?"

"*Wrong!*" the teachers chorused.

"And when your paper came back to you, with one item marked wrong, did you feel proud because it had a 1X at the top? As if the one wrong was more important than the nine right? Wouldn't you have felt better if it had a 9C?"

The teachers nodded their agreement.

"There's definitely something about mistakes or errors that gets our attention," Lucy said. "Media people know about the power of the negative to grab attention. Do you see them reporting much of the good stuff? *Bor*-ing! No, they're in a battle for ratings, so they collect the most sensationally bad things to put before us. But what the behavioral science model has taught us is—what? That very often the negative response reinforces the undesirable behavior by calling attention to it. This means a *gotcha!* response can actually be growing the behavior it seeks to extinguish!"

Thad added, "That's exactly right. Our research at Marine Life Parks, International taught us that it's not a good idea to punish a killer whale and then get in the water with it." This brought laughs from the group.

Lucy said, "I'm going to skip down to the fourth response, the Positive or Whale Done approach. I don't want to say too much about it because we're pretty familiar with it already. Suffice it to say that getting a Whale Done response from someone can turn you around, because it's so unexpected out there in the world. No one expects to be praised or rewarded or recognized for what they do right, so when it comes, it can be very powerful."

Dorothy Hairston smiled and said, "As you all know, I'm the poster child for that!"

This simple, humble statement brought smiles of appreciation from the group.

Lucy continued. "The third one on our list—the Redirection response—is most successful when it ends up with a positive outcome. With the younger children at Wildflower, redirection usually means distracting their attention *away* from what is wrong or undesirable and placing it on something positive. With older students it often takes the form of reasoning out the negative results of the action, and contrasting that with the benefits of doing things right. If you can show children what's in it for *them* to do the right thing, you can usually score a win."

"Another great job," Thad said. "Thank you, Lucy. I want to point out something important about the positive or Whale Done response. That is, to reward in increments. The person you're working with doesn't have to show a perfect performance for you to give a Whale Done. You want to catch them doing something even vaguely in the direction of the right behavior and quickly reinforce it.

"I was giving a series of Whale Done talks to a parent group at my church and from week to week we compared notes. One father said he was really frustrated with his thirteen-year-old son, who teased his younger sister unmercifully. We worked out a plan that had several angles to it.

"First, I told him to ask his daughter not to react when her brother teased her. If she could keep from showing it bothered her, there'd soon be no reward to the brother for teasing her. Second, I told the father to look the other way when the teasing occurred, but as soon as there was a chance to reward the boy's being nice to his sister, to jump on it.

"The following week the father reported the results to the group. When the boy passed some food to his sister after she asked for it, the father said, 'That was nice.' When the boy waited for his sister to catch up with him as they were running for the bus, the father called out, 'Nice job, Tim!' The kid hardly knew what was happening. But the dad kept it up. Every little thing the brother did that was *approximately right* toward treating his sister nicely got reinforced.

"Now, Tim was no dummy. He was thinking, *Hmm, there seems to be some sort of connection here. Every time I'm mean to my sister they ignore me. As soon as I'm decent to her they're all over me. I guess I'll be decent!*"

Maggie looked at her watch. She rose and said, "It looks like our time is about up. Thad and I plan to work out some ways that the school can stay in touch with him and Marine Life Parks, International." Turning to her guest she said, "I know I speak for all of us when I say how much we've appreciated your visit and your spending time with us. Do you have any closing words for us?"

The killer whale trainer stood and looked over the attentive faces of the teachers. As he spoke it was evident that his appreciation of what he had seen at Wildflower School was sincere.

"As I see it, each of you is fulfilling your real promise as educators of young children," he said. "I don't mean you're not already experts in your field; in fact, I know from talking with you that you're very skilled and dedicated. What I mean by fulfilling your real promise is that you're dealing with the very building blocks of character. As you carry out this wonderful Whale Done program you've started here, you are handling a very powerful ingredient—something like TNT. That's the power of goodness that is already down inside each and every child—just waiting to be released into the world.

"How do I know this? Because as a kid I used to be bad. I mean, I *wanted* to be bad. Being good was boring. I was obeying every impulse—and most of them were mischievous. Some of my teachers *said* I was a bad kid, and I was out to prove them right. Sure, I was punished by the teachers and my parents but on the playground with my classmates, I was the cool kid! That's a strong reinforcer!

"As you can see, my teachers were paying far too much attention to what I did wrong, not realizing how reinforcing my new status was scoring with the other children. In reality, had my teachers paid more attention to what the good students were doing right, maybe I would have tried harder to be good as well.

"This experience stuck with me as I grew up and began working killer whales. They too have the reputation of being the "bad kids" of the ocean. I was determined to teach them in a positive way that made them want to do the right thing rather than the wrong thing. I never wanted them to see me as a disciplinarian or as someone they should fear. I wanted them to see me as someone they liked. I was determined to be a good teacher to them.

"So I guess there's a rule," Thad concluded as he turned and wrote on the whiteboard:

You get what you're looking for.

Maggie looked around the room at the teachers sitting silently, many with moist eyes.

Then Dorothy spoke up. "You nailed it, darlin'!"

Maggie Carlson stood before two hundred students who were seated in the school cafeteria eating breakfast. The pictures of leaping killer whales and inflatable replicas of the huge black-and-white creatures hanging from the ceiling had transformed an otherwise utilitarian space into a cheerful atmosphere.

"I have a special Whale Done this morning," Maggie said.

The silence maintained by the assembled small bodies was a testimony to their interest in who would receive the Whale Done certificate.

"Mattie Nichols has earned a Whale Done for going one whole period without hurting anybody," the principal declared.

Around the room Maggie heard boys and girls gasping at her announcement. All eyes were on Mattie—the school bully—as his small figure came forward. A cheer went up from the girls and boys:

"Whaaaaaale, *Done*, Mattie!"

As she gave the boy his certificate, Maggie saw that some of the children who had been Mattie's victims were joining in the praise.

Mattie was returning to his seat when he saw Thad Lacinak gesturing for him to come to the back of the cafeteria.

"Nice going, guy!" Thad told the boy. "Let me see what you got."

As Thad reached for the paper, Mattie started to snatch it away, but then he handed it over. Thad stood there admiring the Whale Done as the principal dismissed the assembly and students and teachers filed out. When most of them were gone, Thad called Maggie over to him and Mattie.

"Dr. Carlson, I just wanted you to join me in congratulating Mattie again for earning a Whale Done, and to see if you had any ideas about how he might earn another one."

Maggie looked at the boy, who was staring at her expectantly. "Well, how was it earning this one, Mattie?" she asked.

"Not bad," the boy said.

"I wonder if you think you could go ... no, I guess ... hm—"

"What?" said Mattie impatiently.

"I was just thinking you might earn another Whale Done by going *two* periods without fighting. But I guess you—"

"I could do that."

"You'd have to stay in your seat the whole time," Maggie warned.

Mattie nodded.

"Okay, let's see what Ms. Middleton tells me after school about how you did." She dismissed the child, and she and Thad began walking to her office.

Later in the day Maggie took Thad to meet with Vicki Middleton and Mattie in Vicki's classroom.

"He did it," Vicki exclaimed proudly. "Mattie went two periods without hurting anyone." Mattie looked away, but it was evident he was enjoying a rare taste of positive attention.

"Nice going, son," said Thad.

"How does it feel to be doing this great?" Maggie asked.

"I like it," said Mattie.

"Let's call your mom and tell her," Maggie said.

The three of them went to her office and phoned Mattie's mother. Somewhat embarrassed, Mattie took the receiver.

"Mom, it's Mattie. I got another Whale Done today. Yeah. Okay." He hung up. "She liked it," he said.

"Think you can go a half day this time?" Thad asked.

The boy nodded.

"What about a full day?"

Mattie said, "I guess so."

After Mattie returned to class, Thad smiled at Maggie.

"That was perfect," he said. "Changing a deeply embedded behavior like this is like turning a big ocean liner. It has to be done slowly and carefully. The kid has all kinds of reinforcements for violence from home, so we have to realize this is counter-intuitive for him. Challenging him with small steps is the way to do it."

"I'm so proud of him already," Maggie said. "I hope I wasn't acting too doubtful there."

"No, that was great. It will make him want to try harder."

Thad's prediction was accurate. After receiving Whale Dones at each morning assembly during the following week, Mattie went a full day without making trouble. When asked what he wanted as a reward for going an entire school week without a fight, he said he wanted to help take care of the crabs in the classroom terrarium. This was an activity Mattie's teacher knew he loved. Before long he had become the leader in charge of the terrarium. By the end of the semester he was stopping fights on the playground.

CHAPTER 13

Passing It On

Two years later

The screaming and loud threats could be heard all the way down the hall. Maggie was in her office with a student, a tall third grader named Karen who was feeling ill. She was talking to the girl's mother on the phone. Through the open door Maggie saw the science teacher, Lucy, leading a small boy by the hand as the child continued his yelling.

"I'm sorry, Ms. McCormack, I'll have to call you back," said Maggie as the teacher and screaming student neared her open door. Maggie hung up and was about to handle the situation, but the young girl rose confidently from her chair and stood in front of the ill-behaved boy.

"You're the new kid," she said in a clear, firm voice. "My name is Karen. What's yours?"

Suddenly subdued, the boy answered, "Desmond."

Karen sat down in the chair beside him. "When I first came here, I used to be like you," she said. "I acted bad then, but I don't anymore, because I found out about Whale Done. You need to calm down, Desmond, because these people are here to help you."

Melted by the girl's kind manner, the boy dissolved in tears.

Karen patted his arm. "It's okay," she said. "Close your eyes, take a breath, and think Whale Done."

Within minutes the situation was resolved and Desmond returned with his teacher to the classroom. Maggie called Karen's mother back and smiled at the girl as she told how she had handled the situation. She hung up and dismissed the child.

From the adjacent office space, Maggie's assistant, Jane, had watched the whole scene. She came and stood in front of Maggie's desk. "Wasn't that something?" she said.

Maggie nodded. "I remember Karen's first day of school, nearly two years ago, like it was yesterday."

"Really?" said Jane. "That was before my time. Tell me about it."

"She got things off to a bang," Maggie said. "She started a fight that first morning. But that was only the beginning. She would throw huge tantrums right in the middle of class, at the slightest provocation. Things would seem fine, then suddenly Karen would become utterly uncontrollable. I saw a lot of her, because teachers were always sending her down here, just like she told Desmond."

"What did you do? When did the turnaround happen?" Jane asked. "I mean, she's like a regular behavior consultant now!"

"The change didn't happen overnight, I can tell you," said Maggie. "Working with Karen, I tried to find out what was behind her anger. I noticed she smelled and always wore filthy oversized clothes, so I investigated her situation. I learned that her parents had recently separated. I did what I could to befriend the child but the episodes, particularly the kicking and hitting of other students, continued almost daily. Karen had no friends; her belligerence drove everyone away."

Maggie smiled suddenly. "It seems funny now, but her calling card back then was noise."

"Noise?"

"Her favorite way of venting her anger was to run out of the classroom and start slamming and kicking the hallway locker doors. You could hear the booms and bangs all over the building. The teachers couldn't stand it. In the first two months of school that child was sent to my office almost daily.

"Then we started the Whale Done program, and when she found herself in a culture of increasing caring and respect, Karen began to change. Her teachers watched her carefully for small actions they could reward—staying in her seat, raising her hand, *not* yelling out. Over months, she earned several Whale Done certificates.

"Then one day one of the teachers brought in an almost new denim jacket as a donation. When I saw it, I immediately thought of Karen. I called her to the office and showed it to her. I said, 'This is a magic jacket. You will be so happy wearing it that you won't want to make trouble anymore.' You should have seen that girl's eyes light up! That was the turning point for Karen. She wore that jacket every day. Her whole demeanor changed and pretty soon she was no longer a problem."

Jane's eyes twinkled. "Do you think it was the jacket that turned her around?"

Maggie smiled. "I think it was what the jacket represented to her. It reminded her that she was someone who'd earned recognition and praise. It reminded her that she mattered."

Maggie and a parent, Lola Tilley, were in the principal's car, on their way to speak to a faculty of a middle school in a nearby district about Wildflower's Whale Done program.

"You were very good to agree to come with me," Maggie said.

"I'm worried how I'll do. I'm pretty nervous," said Lola.

"You'll do fine. As I told you, I think it's so important for teachers to hear about our Whale Done program from the point of view of a parent of one of our students."

"Trey sure is proud of those Whale Dones," Lola said. "Over the past couple of years he's gotten eighteen of them. All but one of them are up on the wall in our front room. He wanted me to paste that first one he got into our family scrapbook."

Maggie drove on in silence for a while. "How are things going with Trey's brother, Albert, these days?" she asked.

Lola Tilley sighed. "Oh, he's still in jail. I worry so about Albert. He's really a good boy at heart."

"And you have a daughter, too. What's her name?"

"Keira. She's four now. Trey says 'Whale Done' every time his sister does something right. I think he's even changing the way I'm being a mom. He doesn't like me yelling at Keira and he keeps wanting me to notice the *good* things she does. He's always telling me, 'You need to give Keira a Whale Done, Mama!' So I've been doing it. And you know what? It works!"

As Maggie drove along, her eyes were glistening. *There it is,* she thought. *Second generation Whale Done!*

The End

Acknowledgments

This book could never have come about without the spiritual guidance and support of our great friend Ken Blanchard. As mentor to groups and organizations around the world, Ken has tirelessly brought the message, "Catch people doing things right". He was our co-author in *Whale Done! The Power of Positive Relationships and Whale Done Parenting; How to Make Parenting A Positive Experience for You and Your Kids.* "Catching people" is not only a central theme of his, it's one he constantly lives himself. Thank you, Ken, for being the spirit behind *The Whale Done School.*

The authors heartily acknowledge Chuck Tompkins, coauthor of *Whale Done!* and *Whale Done Parenting.* With Thad Lacinak, Chuck developed the animal training methods used today in marine parks and described in these books. He continues to be an inspiration in all things Whale Done.

Finally, the authors wish to acknowledge the outstanding contributions of our "two Marthas" of the Ken Blanchard Companies. Martha Lawrence gave us valuable ideas and editorial assistance. Martha Maher contributed to the cover design.

Cindy Zurchin would like to acknowledge all the teachers, students, and families of Pittsburgh Schaeffer Primary School who helped create the first Whale Done school in the nation, with a special thanks to the Whale Done champions: Pam Marmarelli, Ellen Maust, Andrea Germansky, Josh White, Lizz Fulton, Sheree Craighead, Marie Shortt, June Drnevich, Linda Loncaric-Arico, Shellie Hensler, Sharon Schneider, Doris Wall, Lori Blackhurst, Jen Bichler, Jane Bickel, Susan Rooney, Sheila Haiges, Pam Buford, Mark Lucot, Tom Wilson, Robin Ventura, Brice Flenory, Sue Gove, Diane Mead, Justin Brown, Nancy Burns, Reverend Carver, David Malone, Theresa Smith, Representative Dan Deasy, and Mark Roosevelt. Cynthia would also like to thank her husband, John, and her two sons, John Robert and Nicky Zurchin. Finally, she would like to thank her father, Bert, who taught her to help all people, and her mother, Gloria, who taught her to never give up and to fight for what she wanted.

For making him not only want to teach but to design instruction that awakens the best in learners, **James Ballard** thanks all the teachers in his life, in particular those from his high school days at the Rivers School: Clarence Allen, Mr. Gallagher, Mr. Chute, Mr. Ellis, and Mr. Prince. He acknowledges his mentors in his career: Ken Blanchard, Warren Timmermann, Jerry Lynch, Harold Bessell, Uvaldo Palomares, Victor Frankl, Carl Rogers, Thomas Gordon, Ken Miller and Noel ("Speed") Burch. James acknowledges his best friend, Barbara Perman, from whom a "Whale

Done" means most. Very humbly but importantly, he honors his spiritual mentors, Glenn Clark, Rufus Jones, Peter Marshall, Walter Russell, Carl Jung, Brothers Bimmelananda, Ananda Moy, Achalananda and Bhaktananda and Sisters Daya Mata, Tara Mata, Mrinalini Mata and Mukti Mata of Self-Realization Fellowship. Above all, for their ongoing teaching and inspiration in his life, James bows before Mahavatar Babaji, Lahiri Mahasaya, Swami Sri Yukteswar, and his beloved guru-preceptor, Paramahansa Yogananda, author of *Autobiography of A Yogi* and *The Second Coming of Christ.*

Thad Lacinak would especially like to thank his daughter, Michele, who is a constant inspiration to him, his grandson, Joshua, and his mother and father for their guidance and positive influence. Thad would also like to thank and acknowledge his partner, Angi Millwood, for her continuous support in advancing the positive approach to working with people and animals.

About the Authors

Dr. Cynthia R. Zurchin is the assistant superintendent of the Moon Area School District in Moon Township,  Pennsylvania. Previously, she spent twenty-five years in the Pittsburgh public schools where she worked as an elementary and high school principal and administrator on special assignment training new principals, assisting low achieving schools, and integrating arts education programs. She also served as a staff development specialist, middle school assistant principal, and a middle and high school teacher.

Cindy received her doctorate degree in educational leadership from Duquesne University, Pittsburgh, Pennsylvania. She has studied leadership at the Covey Leadership Institute in Utah and has taught in Brisbane, Australia.

Her article, "The Whale Done! School," was published in the March/April 2011 *National Association of Elementary and Secondary School Principal Magazine*.

Cindy regularly speaks and coaches on the *Whale Done!* theme for national and local conferences and institutes. She is a board member for Yoga in Schools and the Education Partnership. She also serves as president of Phi Delta Kappa and as a participant in Leadership Pittsburgh. Earlier in her career she founded Cynthia's School of Dance & Music to teach the love of dance and music to students.

Cindy lives with her husband and two children in Sewickley, Pennsylvania. You can contact her at whaledoneschool@yahoo.com or 412-418-7498.

James Ballard is the principal writer of the Whale Done! series, including *Whale Done! the Power of Positive Relationships, Whale Done Parenting,* and *The Whale Done School.* He lives in Amherst, Massachusetts, and makes his living as an author and consultant. A former teacher, management trainer, and instructional designer, he has contributed many programs on leadership, management, and self-management through change to organizations such as The Ken Blanchard Companies, Life Pilot, and International Speakers Bureau. James has coauthored a number of books with Ken Blanchard, including *Everyone's A Coach, Customer Mania, Whale Done!,* and *Whale Done Parenting.* Ballard's own books include

What's the Rush?, *Mind Like Water*, and *Little Wave and Old Swell*. In 2008 Jim coauthored *No Ordinary Move* with Dr. Barbara Perman, and in 2009 he co-wrote *The Champion; Finding the Most Valuable Person in Your Network* with Frank Agin.

Ballard is a trained life coach (www.lifecrafters.us) and maintains a coaching blog. A meditator for thirty years and a runner for forty, he is a hospice volunteer and Big Brother in the Amherst community. You can email him at jimballard33@gmail.com.

Thad Lacinak is a founder and co-owner of Precision Behavior. In this role, he manages project development and consulting and works to advance animal behavior modification techniques and trainer safety within the zoological community. Thad is also integral to development of the instructional products of the company, teaching positive reinforcement based courses to both zoological and corporate clients.

Previously, Thad retired from a 35-year career at Busch Entertainment Corporation (BEC), as Vice President and Corporate Curator of Animal Training where he directed animal training and enrichment efforts at all U.S. SeaWorld and Busch Gardens Theme Parks.

Since the publication of the New York Time's best-seller, *Whale Done!* in 2001, which sold over a million copies in eighteen languages, Thad continues to present keynote speeches, seminars and workshops globally to major corporations explaining how instituting a Whale Done culture can vastly improve working relationships

Thad can be contacted for keynotes and workshops at tlacinak@precisionbehavior.com. To learn more about Thad and Precision Behavior please visit: www.precisionbehavior.com.

CPSIA information can be obtained
at www.ICGtesting.com
Printed in the USA
LVHW090008160821
695373LV00006B/979